Southern Living®
Cookbook
Library

The
Party Snacks
Cookbook

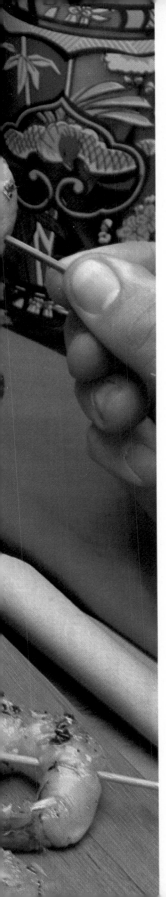

*Cover: (Clockwise) Hot Cocktail Turnovers (page 54);
Kaspin Stuffed Eggs (page 68); Mushrooms Stuffed with
Spinach Soufflé (page 42); Marinated Broccoli (page 62);
Stuffed Cherry Tomatoes (page 80); Shrimp Mousse
(page 139)*

Left: Barbecued Shrimp (page 52)

contents

preface

Tempting party snacks can be the difference between the success and failure of an open house, a reception, or just a casual get-together.

Your selection of snacks will depend on the type of party you're hosting. Appetizers served before a dinner may be quite light and just enough to whet the appetite. Heavier and more substantial snacks are called for if you're hosting a lengthy cocktail party. When planning your party menu, keep in mind that party food should be planned with consideration for variety in color, texture, temperature, and contrast in flavor.

We have included all kinds of party snacks in our collection of over 400 recipes—hot appetizers, cold appetizers, spreads and dips, canapés, dainty party food, and beverages. Many of these foods can be prepared ahead of time and frozen. Spreads and dips actually improve as flavors blend in chilling. Hot appetizers can be made early and kept warm in chafing dishes or on hot trays. Advance preparation of food gives you more free time to spend with your guests.

The perfect snacks are those which are easy to serve and easy to eat. Whether you're serving an intimate group or a large crowd, concentrate on bite-size servings and pick-up foods that can be served with wooden picks or picked up with the fingers.

Chafing Dish Oysters (page 42)

hot appetizers

Tempting hot appetizers take the spotlight for casual get-togethers. Whether it's for a pre-game party or the finale to an evening of bridge, have plenty of appetizers on hand.

When planning your party menu, choose appetizers that will give variety in color, texture, and flavor. Remember that appetizers served before dinner may be quite light, just enough to whet the appetite. More substantial food is called for if you're hosting a lengthy party.

Plan party food that can be prepared ahead of time, giving you more free time to spend with guests. Many hot appetizers can be made early and kept warm in chafing dishes or on hot trays. If your appetizer requires grilling, let your guests do it themselves on a small hibachi. You'll enjoy it more and your guests will, too.

ARTICHOKE CHEESE SQUARES

2 (6-ounce) jars marinated
    artichoke hearts
1 small onion, finely chopped
4 eggs, beaten

6 saltine crackers, crushed
2 cups shredded sharp
    Cheddar cheese

Drain artichoke hearts, reserving about 2 tablespoons marinade. Sauté onion in reserved marinade; drain. Combine onion with artichokes and remaining ingredients, stirring after each addition.

Pour into a greased 8- x 8- x 2-inch baking dish. Bake at 325° for 35 to 40 minutes. Cool thoroughly, and cut into 1-inch squares. Reheat before serving. Yield: 64 (1-inch) appetizer squares.

HOT BACON APPETIZERS

½ pound bacon, cooked
¾ cup shredded pasteurized
    process American cheese
¼ cup butter or margarine,
    softened

2 teaspoons caraway seed
Melba rounds

Crumble bacon; combine with cheese, butter, and caraway seed. Spread on melba rounds. Place on a cookie sheet and broil about 4 inches from source of heat until cheese is melted and bubbling hot. Remove from broiler and serve immediately. Yield: about 4 dozen.

BACON-BOBS

1 (¾-pound) package
    wafer-thin bacon
1 cup Sauterne
¼ cup soy sauce

½ pound chicken livers, cut
    into halves
1 (1-pound) package frozen
    potato bites

Cut bacon slices in half; dip into mixture of Sauterne and soy sauce. Wrap around chicken liver pieces and potato bites. Thread on skewers or fasten each with a wooden pick. Place in a shallow dish and bake at 400° for 25 minutes or until bacon is crisp and golden. Yield: about 5 dozen.

BACON-CHESTNUT APPETIZERS

15 slices bacon, cut
    lengthwise

2 (5-ounce) cans water
    chestnuts, drained (30
    chestnuts)

Wind bacon slices around whole chestnuts; secure with wooden picks. Place on a cookie sheet and bake at 350° for about 25 minutes, until bacon is well done and crisp, turning the chestnuts when half done if necessary. Drain on paper towels and keep warm until serving time. Yield: 2½ dozen.

Hospitality Tea Punch (page 184); Bacon Rollups (below); Frosted Egg Mound (page 130)

BACON ROLLUPS

2 (3-ounce) packages cream
   cheese with chives,
   softened
1 tablespoon milk or
   mayonnaise

25 slices mixed-grain
   sandwich bread, crusts
   removed and slices cut in
   half
25 slices bacon, cut in half

Combine cream cheese and milk, stirring until spreading consistency.

Spread 1 scant teaspoon of cream cheese mixture on each half slice of bread, and roll tightly. Wrap each rollup with bacon, securing with a toothpick.

Place rollups on a broiler pan; bake at 350° for 30 minutes, turning if necessary to prevent overbrowning. Garnish with parsley, if desired. Yield: 50 rollups.

Note: Bacon Rollups may be assembled ahead and frozen. To serve, thaw overnight in refrigerator; bake at 350° for 30 to 40 minutes.

CARAWAY BISCUITS

1 cup all-purpose flour	⅓ cup butter or margarine
1 teaspoon dry mustard	Several drops hot pepper
1 teaspoon salt	sauce
½ cup shredded Swiss cheese	½ teaspoon Worcestershire
(or Swiss and Parmesan	sauce
cheese mixed)	About 3 tablespoons cold
½ teaspoon paprika	water
2 teaspoons caraway seed	

Combine flour, mustard, and salt in a bowl. Stir in cheese, paprika, and caraway seed. Cut in butter until particles are about the size of peas. Sprinkle with hot pepper sauce, Worcestershire sauce, and cold water. Toss lightly with a fork until dough holds together. Form into a ball and roll out on a floured surface into a 13- x 9-inch rectangle. Using a pastry wheel, cut into 1-inch squares. Place on ungreased cookie sheets, sprinkle with a little paprika, and bake at 425° until brown, just about 7 minutes. Do not overbake. Will freeze. Yield: about 8 dozen.

CHEESE BISCUITS

½ pound butter or margarine,	1 egg
softened	1 long loaf white bread, thinly
2 cups shredded sharp	sliced
Cheddar cheese	
1 or 2 dashes of cayenne	
pepper	

Place the first 4 ingredients in small bowl of an electric mixer and beat until fluffy.

Use 1 long loaf white bread. Stack three slices; remove crusts. Cut into quarters. Spread cheese and butter mixture generously between slices; then ice top and sides very thinly. Place on a lightly greased cookie sheet and bake at 350° for 12 to 15 minutes. Serve warm. Yield: 3 dozen.

Note: Biscuits freeze beautifully and require no thawing before baking. To freeze, complete the icing, place biscuits on a flat tray and place uncovered in freezer until firm; then store in freezer container with waxed paper between layers.

CRUNCHY CHEESE BISCUITS

½ cup butter or margarine,	½ teaspoon salt
softened	Hot pepper sauce and
1 cup all-purpose flour	Worcestershire sauce to
1 cup shredded sharp Cheddar	taste
cheese, softened	1 cup rice cereal bits

Blend all ingredients except cereal bits by hand in a bowl until thoroughly mixed. Work in cereal bits. Pinch off into tiny balls about the size of a nickel. Place on an ungreased cookie sheet; press down with a fork and bake at 325° for 10 minutes or until faintly colored. Yield: about 4 dozen.

TINY CHEESE BISCUITS

4½ cups all-purpose flour
½ teaspoon salt
½ to 1 teaspoon cayenne
  pepper

4 cups shredded sharp
  Cheddar cheese
1 pound butter or margarine,
  softened

Combine flour, salt, and cayenne pepper; blend in cheese and butter until smooth. Pat or roll out on a floured surface to about ⅓-inch thickness. Cut with inside of doughnut cutter or other small cutter. (To avoid dough clinging to cutter, dip cutter frequently into cold water.) Place about ⅛ inch apart on an ungreased cookie sheet and bake at 325° for about 15 minutes. Do not allow the biscuits to brown; it's easy to overbake them. Store in an airtight container, placing waxed paper between layers. Freezes beautifully; thaw in closed tin. Yield: about 10 dozen.

SESAME COCKTAIL BISCUITS

1 (3-ounce) package cream
  cheese, softened
½ cup butter or margarine,
  softened
1¼ cups all-purpose flour

½ teaspoon seasoned salt
⅓ cup toasted sesame seed
Coarse (kosher) salt or more
  seasoned salt

Cream cheese and butter together in large bowl of electric mixer until blended. Add flour, ½ teaspoon seasoned salt, and sesame seed. Mix thoroughly. Flour hands lightly and form mixture into a long roll about 1 inch in diameter. Wrap in waxed paper and chill thoroughly.

To bake, slice into ¼-inch-thick rounds; place on a greased cookie sheet and bake at 350° for about 15 minutes or until light golden. While still hot, sprinkle with a few grains of coarse salt or a little seasoned salt. Store in an airtight container; biscuits may be frozen, then thawed in same container. Yield: 7 to 8 dozen.

Note: To toast sesame seed, place in a shallow baking dish and bake at 275° for 25 minutes, shaking the dish a little from time to time.

• *After deciding on the menu for your party, make the grocery list in two parts: things that can be bought and prepared ahead of time or stored, and the perishables that have to be purchased the day of the party.*

GULFPORT CHEESE BALLS

3 egg whites	1 teaspoon parsley flakes
3 cups shredded extra sharp Cheddar cheese	Paprika
	Cornmeal
⅓ cup all-purpose flour	Hot melted shortening or salad
4 dashes of hot pepper sauce	oil
Dash of salt	

Beat egg whites very stiff; add cheese, flour, hot pepper sauce, salt, parsley flakes, and paprika. Roll mixture into small balls and roll in cornmeal. Place balls in a skillet with about ¼ inch hot shortening or salad oil. Turn constantly with long fork. Cook until golden brown. Yield: about 25 to 30 appetizers.

CURRY-COCONUT CHEESE BALLS

2 (8-ounce) packages cream cheese, softened	1⅓ cups flaked coconut
	1½ teaspoons curry powder

Form 64 small cream cheese balls; set aside. Toss coconut with curry powder until well mixed; spread in a thin layer in a shallow baking dish. Toast at 350° for 8 to 12 minutes or until delicately browned. Stir or shake dish often to brown coconut evenly. Cool. Roll cream cheese balls in curry-coconut. Chill until firm. Yield: 64 appetizers.

OLIVE-FILLED CHEESE BALLS

2 tablespoons butter or margarine, softened	½ cup all-purpose flour
	Dash of cayenne pepper
1 cup shredded sharp Cheddar cheese	½ teaspoon celery seed
	2 (3-ounce) jars stuffed olives

Mix butter and cheese until smooth; blend in flour, cayenne pepper, and celery seed. Shape 1 teaspoon of dough around each olive to form a ball. Place on cookie sheets; bake at 400° for 15 minutes. Serve hot or cold.

To freeze, place uncooked balls about ½ inch apart on a cookie sheet (make sure balls do not touch each other); cover with heavy-duty aluminum foil and place in the freezer. After cheese balls are thoroughly frozen, remove from cookie sheet and store in plastic bags in the freezer. To serve, place frozen balls on a cookie sheet. Bake at 400° for 18 to 20 minutes. Yield: about 3 dozen.

OLIVE-CHEESE SNACKS

1 (5-ounce) jar bacon-cheese spread	¾ cup all-purpose flour
	30 medium stuffed green olives
¼ cup butter or margarine	
Dash of hot pepper sauce	
Dash of Worcestershire sauce	

Blend cheese and butter together until light and fluffy. Add hot pepper sauce and Worcestershire sauce; mix well. Stir in flour; mix to form a dough. Shape around olives, using about 1 teaspoon dough for each. Place on an ungreased cookie sheet. Bake at 400° for 12 to 15 minutes or until golden brown. Yield: about 2½ dozen.

OLIVE-CHEESE TIDBITS

½ cup butter or margarine, softened	1¼ cups all-purpose flour
	Dash of salt
1 (5-ounce) jar English Cheddar cheese	48 medium stuffed olives, drained and dried

Cut butter and cheese into flour; add salt. Form into small balls around olives and seal well. Let stand in refrigerator overnight. Bake at 400° for about 15 minutes or until brown. Yield: 4 dozen.

SESAME BALLS

½ cup butter or margarine, softened	Dash of salt and pepper
	Dash of paprika
2 cups shredded process American cheese	Dash of onion powder
1 cup all-purpose flour	Toasted sesame seeds

Combine butter and cheese. Add flour, salt, pepper, paprika, and onion powder; mix well. Form into balls; flatten and dip into toasted sesame seeds. Bake on an ungreased cookie sheet at 375° for 15 to 20 minutes. Yield: about 4 dozen.

PARMESAN CHEESE BITES

1 cup all-purpose flour	½ cup butter or margarine, softened
1 or 2 dashes of cayenne pepper	Evaporated milk or cream
⅔ cup grated Parmesan cheese	

Place flour in a mixing bowl; stir in pepper and cheese. Cut in butter with a pastry blender; then work dough with hands until it holds together. Roll out on a floured surface to ⅓-inch thickness and cut into 1- or 1½-inch squares. (A pastry wheel gives an attractive edge.) Transfer to an ungreased cookie sheet; brush tops with evaporated milk or cream and bake at 350° for 12 to 15 minutes. Do not overbake. Freezes well. Yield: about 2½ dozen.

CHEESIES

1½ cups butter or margarine, softened
1½ pounds sharp Cheddar cheese, shredded
3 cups all-purpose flour
1½ teaspoons salt
¾ teaspoon hot pepper sauce
4½ cups crushed corn flakes

Cream butter; add cheese, flour, and salt. Mix well. Add hot pepper sauce and corn flakes (mixture will be crumbly). Form into small balls and place on a lightly greased cookie sheet. Bake at 350° for 15 to 20 minutes or until dry and lightly browned. Yield: 7 to 8 dozen.

CARAWAY CRISPS

2 cups all-purpose flour
1 teaspoon baking powder
1 teaspoon salt
½ cup butter or margarine
2 tablespoons cream cheese
1 egg, beaten
1 egg white, unbeaten, or milk
Caraway seed
Coarse salt or kosher salt

Combine flour, baking powder, and salt in a bowl. Cut in butter and cream cheese until granular. Add beaten egg and work with fingers until dough is smooth. Chill; then roll out between sheets of waxed paper or on pastry cloth to ¼-inch thickness. Cut into strips 1 x 3 inches. Brush with egg white or milk; sprinkle with caraway seed and salt. Twist each strip and place on an ungreased cookie sheet. Bake at 400° for about 15 minutes or just until golden. Yield: about 3 dozen.

CHEESE-RICE CRISPY

2 cups shredded cheese
1 cup butter or margarine, softened
2 cups all-purpose flour
2 cups crisp rice cereal

Combine cheese and butter; add flour and mix well. Add crisp cereal and mix well. Shape into small balls and place on ungreased cookie sheets. Flatten each ball with a fork and bake at 375° for 10 minutes. Yield: about 5 dozen.

CHEESE CROQUETTES

3 tablespoons melted butter or margarine
¼ cup all-purpose flour
⅔ cup milk
2 egg yolks
½ cup shredded Gruyère cheese
1 cup cubed mild Cheddar cheese
½ teaspoon salt
⅛ teaspoon pepper
¼ teaspoon cayenne pepper
2 to 2½ cups soft breadcrumbs
3 to 4 eggs, beaten
Hot salad oil

Combine butter and flour in a small saucepan, and cook until bubbly. Gradually stir in milk; cook over medium heat, stirring constantly, until smooth and thickened. Add egg yolks, mixing well. Stir in Gruyère cheese, and cook over low heat until melted.

Remove from heat; stir in Cheddar cheese, salt, pepper, and cayenne. Spread evenly in a greased 9-inch square pan. Cool.

Carefully unmold cheese mixture, and cut into 1-inch squares. Coat with breadcrumbs, dip in egg, and coat again with breadcrumbs. Fry in hot oil until golden brown; drain on paper towels. Serve warm. Yield: about 4 dozen.

PARMESAN KISSES

3 egg whites	1 (2½-ounce) jar grated
¼ teaspoon salt	Parmesan cheese
⅛ teaspoon cayenne pepper	Salad oil

Beat egg whites with salt and cayenne pepper until they hold stiff peaks. Fold in cheese. Drop by teaspoonfuls into hot oil. Fry until brown on both sides. Drain on absorbent paper; serve hot. Yield: 2 dozen.

HOT CHEESE LOGS

6 slices thinly sliced bread	4 (1-ounce) wedges Gruyère
3 tablespoons melted butter or	cheese
margarine, divided	1½ teaspoons anchovy paste

Trim bread crusts and cut each slice of bread in half. Brush with half the butter. Cut each cheese wedge into 3 slices. Place a slice of cheese on each piece of bread. Spread cheese with anchovy paste. Roll bread tightly around cheese. Fasten with a wooden pick. Brush with remaining melted butter. Place on a cookie sheet and broil slowly, turning to brown all sides. Yield: 1 dozen.

CHEESE NIBBLERS

1 cup all-purpose flour	½ cup butter or margarine,
1 cup shredded process	softened
American or Cheddar	¼ teaspoon salt
cheese	

Combine all ingredients in a bowl and blend with a pastry blender. Knead in bowl to form a dough. Shape into balls, using 1 scant teaspoonful of dough for each. Place on ungreased cookie sheets. Bake at 350° for 12 to 15 minutes. Dough may be stored in refrigerator and baked as needed. Yield: about 5 dozen.

CHEESE PENNIES

1 (5-ounce) jar process sharp
   American cheese spread
¼ cup shortening

⅔ cup all-purpose flour

Combine all ingredients; mix on medium speed of electric mixer for 20 to 30 seconds. On a lightly floured surface, mold dough into two 8-inch rolls, 1 inch in diameter. (Dough will be soft but not sticky.) Wrap in waxed paper; refrigerate for 2 hours or overnight.

    Cut rolls into ⅛-inch slices; place on ungreased cookie sheets. Bake at 375° for 12 to 15 minutes or until slightly browned. Yield: about 6 dozen.

CHEESE PUFFBALLS

1½ cups shredded sharp
   Cheddar cheese
1 tablespoon all-purpose flour
½ teaspoon paprika

Pepper
3 egg whites, stiffly beaten
Cracker crumbs
Salad oil

Combine cheese, flour, and seasoning. Add beaten egg whites and shape into small balls. Roll in cracker crumbs. Fry in hot oil at 375°. Drain. Serve hot. Yield: 8 servings.

PARMESAN PUFFS

½ cup mayonnaise
¼ cup grated Parmesan
   cheese
1 teaspoon Worcestershire
   sauce

⅛ teaspoon onion salt
2 teaspoons sherry
48 buttery crackers

Combine mayonnaise, cheese, Worcestershire sauce, onion salt, and sherry. Blend. Spread about 1 teaspoonful of mixture on each cracker. Place on broiler pan. Place top of puffs 2 inches from source of heat; broil 2 to 3 minutes or until lightly browned. Yield: 4 dozen.

PARMESAN CHEESE PUFFS

⅔ cup boiling water
1 cup piecrust mix
2 eggs
4 teaspoons grated Parmesan
   cheese

Salad oil
Grated Parmesan cheese

Heat water in a saucepan over medium heat; add piecrust mix and stir quickly until mixture forms a ball around spoon. Remove from heat; add eggs, one at a time, beating well after each addition. Stir in Parmesan cheese. Heat oil (enough to be 2 inches deep) in a skillet. Drop mixture by half teaspoonfuls into hot oil. Fry until brown on both sides. Drain on absorbent paper. Dust with more Parmesan cheese. Yield: 3 dozen.

CHEESE STICKS

1 cup all-purpose flour	½ cup shredded Cheddar
½ teaspoon salt	cheese, softened
⅛ teaspoon cayenne pepper	3 tablespoons commercial
1½ teaspoons baking powder	sour cream
¼ cup butter or margarine,	
softened	

Combine dry ingredients. Cut in butter and cheese with a pastry blender or 2 forks; stir in sour cream. Shape into a ball and chill for 2 hours. On a lightly floured board, roll out dough ⅛ inch thick. Cut into strips 3 x ¼ inches. Bake at 425° for 8 minutes. Yield: 2 to 3 dozen.

CHEESE STRAWS

3½ cups all-purpose flour	1½ cups butter or margarine
¼ teaspoon salt	4 cups shredded sharp
¾ teaspoon cayenne pepper	Cheddar cheese

Combine flour, salt, and pepper in a large bowl. Cut butter into small pieces and blend into dry ingredients with fingers until mixture resembles coarse crumbs. Add cheese and continue blending until dough hangs together and is no longer crumbly.

Work with ¼ of the dough at a time. Roll out to a rectangle ⅓ inch thick; cut into strips ½ inch wide and about 4 inches long, using a pastry wheel or sharp knife. Place on ungreased cookie sheets and bake at 375° for 10 to 12 minutes, only until very lightly browned. (Do not overbake, which is easy to do.) Remove, cool, and store in an airtight container, placing waxed paper between layers. Freezes beautifully. Yield: about 10 dozen.

FAVORITE CHEESE STRAWS

½ cup butter or margarine	½ teaspoon salt
2 cups shredded process	⅛ teaspoon cayenne pepper
American cheese	1½ cups all-purpose flour

Cream butter and cheese together. Add salt and cayenne pepper and work in the flour. Cover and chill for about 1 hour. Roll out about ⅛ inch thick on a lightly floured cloth or board. Cut in sticks about ½ inch wide and 4 inches long with a sharp knife or pastry wheel. Place on ungreased cookie sheets and bake at 375° for 10 to 12 minutes. Yield: about 4 dozen.

SESAME CHEESE STRAWS

2 cups shredded extra sharp
  Cheddar cheese
1 (2¼-ounce) jar sesame seed
½ cup butter or margarine,
  softened

1¼ cups all-purpose flour
1 teaspoon salt
⅛ teaspoon cayenne pepper

Allow shredded cheese to reach room temperature. Toast sesame seed in heavy skillet, stirring constantly over low heat for 20 minutes or until golden brown; cool. Combine cheese, butter, flour, salt, and cayenne pepper; work dough until mixture is thoroughly blended. Add sesame seed. Roll dough to ⅛-inch thickness; cut into 4- x ½-inch strips. Bake at 400° for 12 to 15 minutes or until golden brown; cool on a wire rack. Place in an airtight container. These stay fresh for several weeks. Yield: 5 dozen.

CHEESE SNAPPY WAFERS

1 cup butter or margarine
2 cups all-purpose flour
1 (8-ounce) package sharp
  cheese, shredded

½ teaspoon cayenne pepper
½ teaspoon salt
2 cups crisp rice cereal

Cut butter into flour until texture resembles coarse meal. Mix in cheese, cayenne pepper, and salt. Fold in cereal. Pinch off small pieces, place on an ungreased cookie sheet, and pat flat. Bake at 350° for 15 minutes. Yield: about 5 dozen.

MAGIC BLUE CHEESE WAFERS

¼ cup butter or margarine
3 ounces blue cheese,
  crumbled

1 cup all-purpose flour
4 teaspoons milk
Sesame seeds

Combine butter, cheese, and flour; mix with a pastry blender until mixture is crumbly. Add just enough milk to hold mixture together. Roll up in a cylinder shape, about 1¼ inches in diameter. Wrap in waxed paper or heavy-duty aluminum foil. Place in the freezer for several hours. Cut into ⅛-inch slices. Sprinkle tops of wafers with sesame seed. Bake on an ungreased cookie sheet at 400° for 5 to 6 minutes. Yield: about 4 dozen.

WELCOME COCKTAIL WAFERS

¾ cup butter or margarine
⅔ cup shredded Cheddar
  cheese
½ cup crumbled blue cheese
1 small clove garlic, crushed

1 teaspoon minced fresh
  parsley
1 teaspoon minced chives
2 cups all-purpose flour

Beat butter with Cheddar and blue cheese in large bowl of electric mixer until well blended. Add all other ingredients and beat again. Dust hands lightly with flour and shape into two rolls about 1½ inches in diameter. Chill thoroughly. Slice ⅛ inch thick and bake at 375° for 8 to 10 minutes. Yield: about 6 dozen.

CRESCENT TWISTS

1 (8-ounce) can refrigerated
   crescent dinner rolls
2 teaspoons melted butter or
   margarine

½ cup shredded Cheddar
   cheese
Garlic or onion salt

Separate dinner rolls into 4 rectangles. Press perforations to seal. Brush 2 of the rectangles with melted butter, about 1 teaspoon each; sprinkle with 1 to 2 tablespoons shredded Cheddar cheese. Sprinkle with garlic salt. Place remaining 2 rectangles on top of seasoned rectangles. Cut each crosswise into ten ½-inch strips. Twist each strip 5 to 6 times; place on an ungreased cookie sheet; secure ends by pressing onto sheet. Bake at 375° for 10 to 12 minutes or until golden brown. Serve warm. Yield: 20 appetizers.

YULE DELIGHTS

1 cup butter or margarine,
   softened
4 cups shredded sharp cheese
2 cups all-purpose flour

2 cups finely chopped nuts
1 teaspoon cayenne pepper
2 teaspoons salt

Thoroughly cream butter and cheese together; add other ingredients and mix well. Roll into a long roll and refrigerate for several hours. Slice into thin rounds. Place on a slightly greased cookie sheet and bake at 325° for 20 minutes or until edges brown. Yule rolls may be frozen and baked months later. Yield: about 5 dozen.

OLIVE WHIRLIGIGS

1 cup shredded sharp process
   American cheese
3 tablespoons butter or
   margarine, softened

Dash of cayenne pepper or hot
   pepper sauce
½ cup all-purpose flour
½ cup chopped stuffed olives

Combine cheese, butter, and cayenne pepper; stir in flour. Between sheets of waxed paper, roll to a 10- x 6-inch rectangle about ⅛ inch thick. Sprinkle pastry with chopped olives. Beginning with long side, roll up as for a jelly roll, lifting waxed paper slightly with each turn. Seal edge. Wrap roll in the waxed paper. Chill for at least 1 hour. Cut into ¼-inch slices. Place about 2 inches apart on ungreased cookie sheets; bake at 400° for 10 minutes or until edges are lightly browned. Serve hot. Yield: 3½ dozen.

CHICKEN BALLS

1 pound uncooked chicken breasts	2 tablespoons cornstarch
3 tablespoons chopped onion	½ teaspoon salt
10 water chestnuts	2 tablespoons soy sauce
1 (2½-ounce) can mushrooms, drained	1 tablespoon sherry
	2 egg whites, stiffly beaten
	Salad oil

Bone chicken breasts and put through food grinder with onion, water chestnuts, and mushrooms. Add cornstarch, salt, soy sauce, sherry, and stiffly beaten egg whites. Form into small balls and fry in deep hot oil. Drain and serve warm with wooden picks. Yield: about 4 dozen.

CHICKEN PUFFS

1 (10-ounce) package frozen patty shells, thawed	1 tablespoon lemon juice
1 (4¾-ounce) can chicken spread	2 tablespoons commercial sour cream
1 tablespoon instant minced onion	3 tablespoons grated Parmesan cheese

Roll each patty shell into a 3-inch square on a floured board. With a sharp knife, cut each square in half diagonally. Place triangles on a cookie sheet. Bake at 400° for 10 minutes or until golden brown. Combine chicken spread, onion, lemon juice, sour cream, and cheese. Split each triangle horizontally and fill with chicken mixture. Return to oven for 2 minutes. Serve hot. Yield: 1 dozen.

BUTTER-HONEY CHICKEN TIDBITS

6 large broiler-fryer chicken thighs, boned	1 teaspoon teriyaki sauce
¼ cup melted butter or margarine	1 teaspoon seasoned salt
¼ cup honey	½ teaspoon garlic salt
	¼ teaspoon pepper
	½ cup sesame seeds, toasted

Rinse chicken thighs and pat dry. Cut each thigh into 6 to 8 pieces. Refrigerate 8 hours.

Combine butter, honey, and teriyaki sauce in a small saucepan; stir well. Bring to a boil; remove from heat, and set aside.

Sprinkle chicken pieces with seasoned salt, garlic salt, and pepper. Dip each chicken piece into honey mixture, and coat with sesame seeds. Place chicken pieces on a cookie sheet. Bake at 350° for 30 minutes, turning once to brown evenly. Reheat remaining honey mixture, and serve with chicken tidbits. Yield: 12 appetizer servings.

CHICKEN ALMOND SWIRLS

1 (8-ounce) can refrigerated
   crescent dinner rolls
1 (4¾-ounce) can chicken
   spread
1 tablespoon diced toasted
   almonds

1 tablespoon mayonnaise
½ teaspoon lemon juice
Seasoned salt

Separate dough into 4 rectangles; press along perforations to seal. Combine remaining ingredients; spread on rectangles. Roll up each rectangle, jelly-roll fashion, starting with long side. Slice each roll into 8 slices. Place cut side down on a greased cookie sheet. Bake at 375° for 12 to 15 minutes or until golden brown. Serve warm. Yield: about 2½ dozen.

LUAU BITS

10 water chestnuts, cut into
   halves
5 chicken livers, cut into
   quarters

10 slices bacon, cut into
   halves
¼ cup soy sauce
2 tablespoons brown sugar

Wrap water chestnuts and chicken livers in bacon slices. Secure bacon slices with wooden picks. Marinate in mixture of soy sauce and brown sugar for 4 hours. Broil about 3 inches from source of heat until bacon is crisp. Yield: about 1½ dozen.

CHERRY-SAUCED CHICKEN WINGS

3 pounds chicken wings
1 (16-ounce) can pitted dark
   sweet cherries
¼ cup firmly packed brown
   sugar
2 teaspoons grated fresh
   gingerroot, or ½ teaspoon
   ground ginger

1 small clove garlic, minced
½ cup soy sauce
¼ cup port
2 tablespoons lemon juice

Cut off and discard the small wing tips of chicken wings. Cut between the main and second wing joints to make 2 pieces from each wing. Place chicken in a bowl. Place cherries with syrup in a blender and blend until smooth. Add remaining ingredients. Pour over chicken wings and marinate 2 to 3 hours, turning occasionally. Drain, reserving marinade. Place chicken wings in a single layer in baking dish. Bake at 450° for 10 minutes. Turn and bake for an additional 10 minutes. Reduce temperature to 350°. Continue to bake 20 minutes longer or until tender, brushing 2 or 3 times with reserved cherry marinade. Serve warm. Yield: about 3 dozen.

Note: Remaining marinade may be thickened with 2 tablespoons cornstarch to serve as a dipping sauce.

POLYNESIAN CHICKEN WINGS

1 pound chicken wings
1 (8-ounce) jar sweet-sour
   salad dressing

Cut off and discard the small wing tips of chicken wings. Cut between the main and second wing joints to make 2 pieces from each wing.

Dip chicken portions in sweet-sour salad dressing. Arrange pieces so that they do not touch on a heavy-duty aluminum foil-lined cookie sheet. Bake at 325° for 1 hour, basting occasionally with the sauce, so that they are golden brown. Do not raise the heat or the meat will brown too quickly. Keep chicken warm in a chafing dish. Yield: 12 servings.

CORN FLINGS

1 (8-ounce) package corn
   muffin mix
4 frankfurters, thinly sliced

2 teaspoons oregano
1½ cups shredded Cheddar
   cheese

Prepare corn muffin mix according to package directions. Spread in a greased 15- x 10½-inch pan and arrange sliced frankfurters over the mix. Top with oregano and bake at 400° for 15 minutes.

Sprinkle cheese over hot bread and place under broiler until cheese bubbles, about 3 minutes. Cut into squares to serve. Yield: about 25 servings.

HOT CORNED BEEF BALLS

2 (12-ounce) cans corned
   beef, flaked
1 medium onion, chopped
1 tablespoon minced parsley
½ cup melted butter or
   margarine
1 cup all-purpose flour
1 teaspoon dry mustard

1 teaspoon salt
1 cup milk
1 (16-ounce) can chopped
   sauerkraut, well drained
2 eggs, beaten
¼ cup water
Fine breadcrumbs
Hot salad oil

Sauté corned beef, onion, and parsley in butter 5 minutes. Stir in flour, mustard, and salt; gradually add milk. Cook, stirring constantly, until thickened. Stir in sauerkraut, mixing well. Chill about 30 minutes. Shape into ½-inch balls.

Combine eggs and water in a small dish. Dip corned beef balls in egg, and coat with breadcrumbs. Refrigerate at least 1 hour. Cook in deep hot oil about 2 minutes or until golden brown. Serve hot. Yield: about 7 dozen.

Note: Corned beef balls may be made in advance and frozen.

CORNED BEEF SPREAD PUFF

1 egg white
¼ cup shredded sharp
  Cheddar cheese
⅛ teaspoon salt
⅛ teaspoon paprika

¼ cup mayonnaise
24 melba rounds
1 (4½-ounce) can corned beef
  spread

Whip or beat egg white until stiff; fold in cheese, salt, paprika, and mayonnaise. Spread melba rounds with corned beef spread. Top with egg white mixture and broil until puffs are golden brown, about 5 minutes. Serve hot. Yield: 2 dozen.

SNACK SQUARES

1 (8-ounce) can refrigerated
  crescent dinner rolls
1 (4½-ounce) can corned beef
  spread
½ teaspoon prepared
  horseradish

2 thin slices red onion,
  separated into rings
4 slices pasteurized process
  American cheese

Remove rolls from package, but do not separate along diagonal perforation. On a lightly floured board, roll each of the 4 pieces into 3½- x 7-inch rectangles. Combine corned beef spread and horseradish; spread mixture on half of each rectangle, leaving ½ inch border of dough uncovered. Place onion rings on top of filling and fold rectangle in half, pinching edges to seal in filling. Bake at 375° for 30 minutes. Top each square with a slice of cheese and continue baking for another 5 minutes. Quarter and serve. Yield: 16 appetizers.

CRAB APPETIZERS

1 pound crabmeat
1 tablespoon grated onion
¼ cup melted butter or
  margarine
¼ cup all-purpose flour
1 cup milk
1 egg yolk, beaten

½ teaspoon Worcestershire
  sauce
¼ teaspoon salt
Dash of pepper
¾ cup dry breadcrumbs
Salad oil

Remove any shell or cartilage from crabmeat. Sauté onion in butter; blend in flour. Add milk gradually and cook until thick, stirring constantly. Combine egg yolk, Worcestershire sauce, and seasonings. Stir a little of the hot sauce into egg yolk; add to remaining sauce, stirring constantly. Add crabmeat; blend into a paste and cool. Shape teaspoonfuls of crab mixture into small balls. Roll in crumbs. Fry at 375° in a basket in deep oil for 2 minutes or until brown. Drain on absorbent paper. Serve on wooden picks. Yield: about 7 dozen.

CRAB DABS

2 (6½- or 7½-ounce) cans
   crabmeat, drained
⅓ cup soft breadcrumbs
2 tablespoons dry sherry
1 teaspoon chopped chives

1 teaspoon dry mustard
¼ teaspoon salt
10 slices bacon, cut into
   thirds

Remove any remaining shell or cartilage from crabmeat; chop crabmeat. Combine all ingredients except bacon. Mix thoroughly. Chill for 30 minutes. Shape tablespoon-size portions of crabmeat into small rolls. Wrap bacon around crab rolls and secure with a wooden pick. Place crab rolls on a broiler pan. Broil about 4 inches from source of heat for 8 to 10 minutes. Turn carefully. Broil 4 to 5 minutes longer or until bacon is crisp. Yield: 2½ dozen.

HOT CREAMED CRAB

1 (8-ounce) package cream
   cheese, softened
½ cup mayonnaise
1 tablespoon lemon juice
½ teaspoon Worcestershire
   sauce
1 teaspoon all-purpose flour
Dash of cayenne pepper

1 (7½-ounce) can crabmeat,
   drained and shredded
⅓ cup slivered toasted
   almonds
Salt to taste
Crackers or melba toast

Beat cheese until smooth in small bowl of electric mixer. Add mayonnaise, lemon juice, Worcestershire sauce, flour, and cayenne pepper; beat again until smooth. Fold in crabmeat, almonds, and salt. Turn into a covered flameproof casserole dish and bake at 300° for 20 minutes. Place over heat (candle or other heating device), or turn into a chafing dish and keep warm until serving time. This is a very delicately flavored mixture and should be served with unsalted crackers or plain melba toast. Yield: 2½ cups.

CRAB OR SHRIMP PUFFS

2 (6½- or 7-ounce) cans
   crabmeat or shrimp
1 cup finely chopped celery
½ cup mayonnaise or salad
   dressing

2 tablespoons chopped onion
2 tablespoons chopped sweet
   pickle
Salt to taste
Puff Shells

Drain crabmeat or shrimp. Combine all ingredients except Puff Shells. Mix thoroughly. Cut tops from Puff Shells. Fill each with approximately 2 teaspoonfuls of salad. Yield: about 4½ dozen.

Puff Shells:

½ cup boiling water
¼ cup butter or margarine
Dash of salt

½ cup all-purpose flour
2 eggs

Combine boiling water, butter, and salt in a saucepan; bring mixture to a boil. Add flour and stir vigorously until mixture forms a ball and leaves the sides of pan. Remove from heat. Add eggs, one at a time, beating thoroughly after each addition. Continue beating until a stiff dough is formed. Drop by level teaspoonfuls onto a well-greased cookie sheet. Bake at 450° for 10 minutes. Reduce heat to 350° and bake for 10 additional minutes. Yield: about 4½ dozen.

CRAB NEWBURG APPETIZER

1 pound crabmeat, fresh or
  canned
4 hard-cooked eggs, grated
1 small onion, grated
Salt to taste
Cayenne pepper or hot pepper
  sauce
2 tablespoons butter or
  margarine

2 tablespoons all-purpose flour
2 cups milk
2 cups shredded Cheddar
  cheese
Miniature pastry shells or
  melba toast

Combine crabmeat, eggs, onion, salt, and cayenne pepper.
Melt butter in top of double boiler; add flour and blend until smooth. Add milk and cook until mixture thickens. Add cheese; stir and cook until cheese blends with sauce. Add crabmeat mixture and cook until hot. Serve in pastry shells or with melba toast. Yield: 20 to 25 servings.

CRABMEAT ROLLS

½ cup half-and-half
1 egg
2 sprigs parsley, stemmed
2 celery tops
Salt
½ teaspoon pepper
Dash of cayenne pepper

3 slices bread, crumbled and
  divided
1 (6-ounce) can crabmeat,
  packed in water or
  6 ounces fresh crabmeat
10 slices bacon

Put half-and-half, egg, parsley, celery tops, salt, pepper, cayenne pepper, and half the bread in a blender. Cover and blend about 1 minute or until mixture is smooth. Empty into a bowl. Flake crabmeat and combine with blended mixture along with the rest of the crumbled bread. Shape into 10 small cakes. Wrap each in a slice of bacon. Broil on all sides until bacon is crisp. Yield: 10 appetizers.

CRABMEAT MARYLAND

6 tablespoons butter or
  margarine, divided
3 tablespoons all-purpose flour
2 cups milk
1 pound crabmeat
½ cup whipping cream or
  half-and-half

Salt, pepper, and paprika
¼ cup dry sherry
Lemon juice
Toast points or melba rounds

Melt 4 tablespoons butter in top of double boiler placed over direct low heat. Blend in flour; gradually add milk, stirring constantly until thick and smooth.

Place pan over hot water, cover, and cook for about 5 minutes. Add crabmeat (which has been carefully picked over), stirring gently to avoid breaking lumps. When heated through, carefully stir in cream and remaining 2 tablespoons butter. Season with salt, pepper, and paprika. Add sherry and lemon juice to taste. Keep heat low until serving time; then transfer to a chafing dish. May be served over toast points or with melba rounds for dipping. Yield: 8 servings.

DATE WHIRL-UPS

1 (8-ounce) package pitted
  dates
32 pecans
½ pound thinly sliced cooked
  ham

1 (8-ounce) can refrigerated
  crescent dinner rolls
¼ cup finely shredded
  Cheddar cheese

Stuff each date with a pecan. Cut ham slices into strips the same width as the dates and wrap a strip around each stuffed date. Roll each half of refrigerated dough (4 triangles), on a lightly floured board, into a 13- x 6-inch rectangle. Sprinkle with cheese. Cut into fourths lengthwise and crosswise. Place a stuffed date on each piece of dough and roll up. Place on an ungreased cookie sheet, seam side down. Bake at 375° for 10 to 13 minutes or until lightly browned. Serve hot. Yield: about 2½ dozen.

CARAMEL FONDUE

2 (10-ounce) jars caramel
  topping
¼ cup butter or margarine
Angel food cake cubes
Pound cake cubes
Marshmallows
Pineapple chunks

Banana chunks
Apple wedges
Mandarin orange sections
Maraschino cherries
Flaked coconut, toasted
Chopped salted peanuts

Heat caramel topping and butter in a saucepan over low heat. Stir until butter is melted and sauce is smooth. Serve in a fondue pot or chafing dish. Spear cake cubes, marshmallows, or fruit on forks; dip in sauce, then in coconut or nuts. Yield: about 2½ cups.

BRANDIED CHOCOLATE ROYALE

1 tablespoon cornstarch	2 tablespoons brandy
2 tablespoons half-and-half	Pound cake, cut into 1-inch
1 tablespoon salad oil	squares
1 teaspoon instant coffee	Marshmallows
granules	Apples, cubed
Dash of ground cinnamon	
1 cup milk	
1 (6-ounce) package	
semisweet chocolate	
morsels	

Combine cornstarch, half-and-half, and salad oil in top of double boiler. Blend in coffee granules, cinnamon, and milk. Cook over medium heat, stirring constantly, until slightly thickened. Add chocolate morsels and brandy. Cook, stirring constantly, until smooth.

Transfer to a fondue pot; keep warm while serving. Dip pound cake squares, marshmallows, or apples into chocolate. Yield: about 2 cups.

Brandied Chocolate Royale (above)

CHOCOLATE FONDUE

1 (6-ounce) package
   semisweet chocolate
   morsels
½ cup light corn syrup

1 teaspoon vanilla extract
Dash of salt
Marshmallows
Assorted fruit

Combine all ingredients except marshmallows and fruit over hot (not boiling) water; stir until chocolate melts and mixture is smooth. Remove from heat; keep warm over hot water. Dip marshmallows or fruit on wooden picks into chocolate fondue. If desired, use drained canned pineapple cubes, drained mandarin oranges, canned black cherries, banana chunks, fresh apple slices, or drained canned fruits for salads, cut into chunks. Yield: about ¾ cup.

SWISS FONDUE

4 cups shredded Swiss cheese
¼ cup all-purpose flour
1 clove garlic, halved
2 cups Sauterne
½ teaspoon salt
½ teaspoon Worcestershire
   sauce

Dash of ground nutmeg
French bread, raw vegetables,
   cooked ham cubes, or
   cooked shrimp

Toss together cheese and flour. Rub inside of saucepan with garlic; discard garlic. Add wine, and heat until bubbles rise. Over low heat, add cheese, ½ cup at a time, stirring after each addition until cheese is melted. Add salt, Worcestershire sauce, and nutmeg. Transfer to a fondue pot. Serve with cubes of French bread, raw vegetables, cooked ham cubes, or cooked shrimp. Yield: 3½ cups.

SAVORY SWISS FONDUE

1 clove garlic, cut in half
4 cups shredded Swiss cheese
Dash of salt
Dash of pepper
Dash of ground nutmeg
1 cup dry white wine

¾ cup cold water, divided
¼ cup cornstarch
Crackers
Cooked meatballs
Cooked ham cubes
Cooked whole shrimp

Rub bottom and sides of a deep ovenproof dish or flameproof glass saucepan with garlic. Discard garlic. Add cheese, seasonings, wine, and ½ cup cold water. Cook over medium heat, stirring constantly, just until cheese is melted. (Cheese and liquid will not be blended.) Combine cornstarch and remaining ¼ cup cold water until smooth. Using a wire whisk, stir cornstarch mixture into melted cheese and wine. Continue cooking over medium heat for about 5 minutes or until fondue is thick and creamy. To serve, keep hot in a chafing dish or over a candle warmer. Serve with crackers, cooked meatballs, cooked ham cubes, or cooked whole shrimp. Yield: about 3 cups.

PIZZA FONDUE

½ pound ground beef
1 small onion, chopped
1 tablespoon melted butter or
  margarine
2 (10-ounce) cans pizza
  sauce
1 tablespoon cornstarch
1½ teaspoons fennel seeds
1½ teaspoons oregano

¼ teaspoon garlic powder
1 (10-ounce) package Cheddar
  cheese, shredded
1 cup shredded mozzarella
  cheese
1 (1-pound) loaf French bread,
  cut into 1-inch cubes

Sauté ground beef and onion in butter until done. Combine pizza sauce, cornstarch, fennel seeds, oregano, and garlic powder; add to ground beef mixture. Cook over medium heat until mixture thickens and bubbles; add cheeses, a third at a time, stirring well after each addition.

Transfer mixture to fondue pot. Toast bread cubes until lightly browned, and serve with fondue. Yield: about 6 cups.

SLOPPY JOE FONDUE

1 (15¼-ounce) can barbecue
  sauce and beef for sloppy
  Joes
½ teaspoon instant minced
  onion
½ teaspoon oregano or
  marjoram

1 cup shredded process
  American cheese
French bread cubes

Combine sloppy Joe mixture, onion, seasoning, and cheese; heat, stirring constantly, until cheese melts. Serve with bread cubes. Serve in a chafing dish, fondue pot, or casserole dish over a candle warmer. Yield: 1¾ cups.

HAM FONDUE

2 (4½-ounce) cans deviled
  ham
½ cup cream of mushroom
  soup, undiluted

½ cup commercial sour cream
2 tablespoons sherry
French bread cubes

Combine deviled ham and soup in the top of a double boiler; heat to boiling over direct heat, stirring occasionally. Place over boiling water; stir in sour cream and sherry. Cover and heat until warm. Serve in a fondue pot over warmer. Serve with French bread cubes. Yield: about 2 cups.

HOT CRAB FONDUE

1 (5-ounce) jar process sharp
  cheese spread
1 (8-ounce) package cream
  cheese
1 (7½-ounce) can Alaskan
  king crabmeat, drained and
  flaked

½ cup half-and-half
½ teaspoon Worcestershire
  sauce
¼ teaspoon garlic salt
¼ teaspoon cayenne pepper
French bread cubes

Melt cheese spread and cream cheese in top of a double boiler. Stir in remaining ingredients (except bread), and heat thoroughly. Pour into a fondue pot and serve warm with cubes of French bread. Yield: about 3 cups.

SHRIMP FONDUE

1 clove garlic
1 (10¾-ounce) can cream of
  shrimp soup, undiluted
1 cup finely shredded Swiss
  cheese

2 tablespoons dry white wine
Rye or French bread, unsliced

Rub chafing dish or top of double boiler with garlic; discard garlic. Add soup and cheese; heat until cheese melts. Stir in wine. Cut bread into 1½-inch squares. To serve, spear a piece of bread with a long fork and dip into hot cheese mixture. Yield: about 1¾ cups.

SHRIMP-CHEESE FONDUE

1 (10¾-ounce) can cream of
  shrimp soup, undiluted
2 teaspoons instant minced
  onion
2 cups shredded Swiss cheese

1 (4½-ounce) can shrimp,
  drained and diced
¼ cup dry sherry
Raw vegetables or breadsticks

Heat soup and onion in a saucepan over low heat. Add cheese and stir until cheese is melted. Add shrimp and sherry. Transfer to a fondue pot. Serve with raw vegetables or breadsticks. Yield: 2¾ cups.

COCKTAIL FRANKFURTERS

¾ cup prepared mustard
1 cup currant jelly

8 to 10 frankfurters

Combine mustard and jelly in a chafing dish or double boiler. Diagonally slice frankfurters into bite-size pieces. Add to sauce and heat through. Yield: 10 servings.

FRITOSBURGERS

2 eggs, beaten
2 tablespoons cornstarch
1 tablespoon soy sauce
1 medium onion, finely
  chopped or grated

⅛ teaspoon pepper
3 cups corn chips, crumbled
1 pound lean ground beef
1 teaspoon Ac'cent

Combine eggs, cornstarch, soy sauce, onion, and pepper; mix well. Add corn chips; stir and allow to stand for 20 minutes. Crumble beef; add Ac'cent and mix well. Add beef to egg mixture. Shape into 1-inch balls; place on a heavy-duty aluminum foil-covered cookie sheet and broil until brown. Remove from heat; serve with wooden picks. Yield: about 2½ dozen.

FRUITY BOBS

1 medium banana
1 (8-ounce) can pineapple
  chunks, drained
1 (11-ounce) jar mandarin
  orange sections, drained

1 (8-ounce) jar maraschino
  cherries, drained
1 (8-ounce) jar honey
Flaked coconut (optional)

Peel banana and cut into ½-inch slices. Alternate fruit on skewers, topping with a cherry. Brush with honey and place on top rack of grill. Cook at low to medium heat until fruit is thoroughly heated. If desired, roll honey-coated fruit skewers in flaked coconut before grilling. Yield: 6 to 8 servings.

HAM PIN-UPS

2 (4-ounce) packages cooked
  sliced ham
2 (8-ounce) cans refrigerated
  crescent rolls

Barbecue sauce (optional)

Separate slices of ham. Roll strips of crescent rolls out flat. Do not separate triangular pieces. Place slices of ham lengthwise on top of dough, overlapping pieces slightly for continuity. Roll ham into dough, jelly-roll style. Cut rolled dough into slices, ½ inch thick. Place on top rack of grill. Cook, turning once, at medium heat until biscuits are puffy and golden brown (about 8 to 10 minutes). If desired, sprinkle Pin-Ups with barbecue sauce after they have been turned on grill. Yield: 10 to 15 servings.

DEVILED HAM TRIANGLES

1 (8-ounce) can refrigerated
    crescent dinner rolls
1 (4½-ounce) can deviled
    ham

¼ cup drained, crushed
    pineapple

Unroll dough and separate into eight triangles along perforated edges. Combine deviled ham and pineapple. Place two mounds of mixture, about ½ inch apart, in the center of each of four triangles. Top each with a second triangle; press dough together around edges and in between the two mounds of filling. Cut each in half, in between the two mounds of filling, to form two smaller filled triangles. Place triangles on an ungreased cookie sheet and press edges of triangles with a fork to seal well. Bake at 375° for 15 minutes or until golden brown. Serve warm or cold. Yield: 8 triangles.

MYSTERY HORS D'OEUVRES

2 medium onions, finely
    chopped
2 tablespoons butter or
    margarine
Fresh parsley, chopped
2 medium tomatoes, chopped

1 tablespoon Worcestershire
    sauce
Pinch of cayenne pepper
Salt and pepper to taste
2 or 3 eggs, beaten
Strips of buttered toast

Sauté onion in butter with chopped parsley until faintly golden brown. Add tomatoes, Worcestershire sauce, cayenne pepper, salt, and pepper. Add eggs and scramble. Serve hot on strips of buttered toast. Yield: 6 to 8 servings.

SNACK KABOBS

4 slices bacon, quartered
1 (7-ounce) package frozen
    small crab puffs, partially
    thawed
1 cooked chicken breast,
    boned and cut into chunks
1 avocado, cut into chunks
16 pineapple chunks

2 bananas, cut into thick
    slices
Commercial Italian salad
    dressing

String meat on short skewers alternately with fruit. Brush with salad dressing. Grill over hot coals, turning once and basting with dressing. Yield: 16 kabobs.

LIVERWURST-ONION CUPS

1 (4¾-ounce) can liverwurst
   spread
1 tablespoon commercial sour
   cream
½ teaspoon lemon juice
½ cup crumbled French fried
   onions

1 (8-ounce) can refrigerated
   crescent dinner rolls
Commercial sour cream

Combine liverwurst spread, sour cream, lemon juice, and onions. Unroll crescent rolls, and cut into four rectangles. Cut each rectangle into six equal pieces; roll each piece into a ball and place one in each of 24 small (1¾-inch) ungreased muffin cups. Press dough out to uniform thickness to cover bottom and sides of muffin cups, nearly to tops of cups. Fill with about 1 teaspoon liverwurst spread mixture, level with edge of dough. Top each with small dab of sour cream. Bake at 375° for 15 minutes. Serve warm. Yield: 2 dozen.

Note: Dough cups may be shaped ahead and kept covered in refrigerator an hour or so before filling and baking.

LOBSTER BOATS

½ pound fresh or frozen
   cooked lobster meat
24 fresh mushrooms,
   approximately 1½ inches in
   diameter
¼ cup cream of mushroom
   soup, undiluted
2 tablespoons soft bread-
   crumbs

2 tablespoons mayonnaise or
   salad dressing
¼ teaspoon Worcestershire
   sauce
⅛ teaspoon hot pepper sauce
Dash of pepper
Grated Parmesan cheese

Thaw frozen lobster meat. Drain lobster meat and remove any remaining shell or cartilage; chop meat. Rinse and dry mushrooms; remove stems. Combine soup, breadcrumbs, mayonnaise, seasonings, and lobster. Stuff each mushroom cap with 1 tablespoon lobster mixture. Sprinkle with cheese. Place mushrooms on a well-greased cookie sheet. Bake at 400° for 10 to 15 minutes or until lightly browned. Yield: 2 dozen.

MACARONI APPETIZERS

2 cups small shell macaroni,
   uncooked

Salad oil for frying
Seasoned salt

Cook macaroni according to package directions, but cook only 6 minutes. Drain. Dry thoroughly on absorbent paper. Deep fry at 375° until golden brown (about 8 minutes). Drain. Turn onto absorbent paper. Sprinkle with salt to taste. Stir well with a fork. Yield: about 2½ dozen.

Meatball Delight (below)

MEATBALL DELIGHT

1½ pounds ground beef
¾ cup uncooked regular oats
1 teaspoon salt
1 teaspoon garlic salt
2 (8-ounce) cans tomato
   sauce
All-purpose flour

Salad oil
1 cup chili sauce
1½ cups water
1 large onion, thinly sliced
1 large green pepper, thinly
   sliced
Hot cooked rice (optional)

Combine ground beef, oats, salt, garlic salt, and 1 can tomato sauce; shape into 1-inch meatballs, and roll each in flour. Brown meatballs in hot oil in a large skillet.

Combine remaining tomato sauce, chili sauce, water, onion, and green pepper; stir well, and pour over meatballs. Cover and simmer 30 minutes over low heat.

Transfer to a chafing dish set on low heat. Serve over rice, if desired. Yield: 4 to 6 servings.

BURGUNDY BEEF BALLS

- 1/3 cup water
- 1 slice white bread, toasted
- 1 pound ground beef
- 1 egg
- 1/8 teaspoon ground nutmeg
- 1 teaspoon salt
- 1/4 cup finely chopped onion
- 1 tablespoon salad oil
- 3 tablespoons all-purpose flour
- 2 cups water
- 2/3 cup Burgundy
- 1/2 teaspoon salt
- 1 tablespoon light brown sugar

Pour 1/3 cup water over toast and mix well. Add ground beef, egg, nutmeg, salt, and onion; mix until blended. Shape mixture into 45 small balls, allowing 1 rounded teaspoonful for each; brown in salad oil. Remove meatballs from pan and set aside.

Measure drippings and return 2 tablespoons to pan; add flour and stir until browned. Stir in 2 cups water until smooth; add wine, salt, and brown sugar. Cook slowly, stirring constantly, for 20 minutes. Add meatballs and cook just until heated through. Yield: 45 meatballs.

CHAFING DISH MEATBALLS

- 1 pound ground beef
- 1/2 cup dry breadcrumbs
- 1/3 cup minced onion
- 1/4 cup milk
- 1 egg
- 1 tablespoon chopped parsley
- 1 teaspoon salt
- 1/8 teaspoon pepper
- 1/2 teaspoon Worcestershire sauce
- 1/4 cup shortening
- 1 (12-ounce) bottle chili sauce
- 1 (10-ounce) jar grape jelly

Combine ground beef, breadcrumbs, onion, milk, egg, parsley, salt, pepper, and Worcestershire sauce; gently shape into 1-inch balls. Melt shortening in a large skillet; brown meatballs. Remove meatballs from skillet; drain fat. Heat chili sauce and jelly in skillet until jelly is melted, stirring constantly. Add meatballs and stir until coated. Simmer for 30 minutes. Serve hot in a chafing dish. Yield: 5 dozen.

GOURMET MEATBALLS

- 1 (8-ounce) package liver sausage
- 1 egg, beaten
- 1/4 pound ground beef
- 1 cup breadcrumbs
- 1/4 cup catsup
- 1/2 teaspoon salt
- All-purpose flour
- 1/4 cup melted butter or margarine
- 1/2 (1 3/8-ounce) package dry onion soup mix
- 1 cup hot water

Combine liver sausage and egg; add ground beef, breadcrumbs, catsup, and salt; mix just until mixture is uniform. Shape into balls the size of a walnut. Roll in flour and fry in butter until brown. Sprinkle with soup mix. Pour hot water over meatballs. Simmer for 15 minutes. Serve hot. Yield: about 4 dozen.

YORKSHIRE MEATBALLS

1½ pounds ground beef	1 tablespoon water
¼ cup catsup	1½ cups all-purpose flour
1 (1⅜-ounce) package onion soup mix	1½ teaspoons baking powder
1 tablespoon instant minced parsley	1 teaspoon salt
¼ teaspoon pepper	4 eggs, beaten
1 egg, beaten	3 tablespoons melted butter
	¾ cup milk
	Cheese Sauce

Combine first 7 ingredients. Shape into 24 meatballs. Place meatballs in a greased 13- × 9- × 2-inch baking dish; set aside.

Combine flour, baking powder, and salt. Combine 4 eggs, butter, and milk; stir in dry ingredients all at once, mixing just until smooth. Pour over meatballs. Bake at 300° for 30 to 40 minutes. Serve with Cheese Sauce. Yield: about 8 servings.

Cheese Sauce:

¾ pound process American cheese, cubed	1¼ teaspoon Worcestershire sauce
⅓ cup milk	

Combine all ingredients in a saucepan. Cook over medium heat, stirring constantly, until cheese is melted. Yield: 1½ cups.

Photograph for this recipe on page 154

MINI-MEATBALLS

1 pound ground pork sausage	1 (5-ounce) can water chestnuts
¼ pound ground beef	2 cups commercial barbecue sauce
1 egg, slightly beaten	
¼ cup dry breadcrumbs	

Place pork sausage and ground beef in a bowl; add egg and breadcrumbs; mix well. Cut each water chestnut into 4 to 6 small pieces. Shape a scant tablespoonful of meat around each piece. Roll in palms of hands to make balls. Place meatballs in an unheated skillet; cook slowly, turning carefully until browned on all sides. Transfer meatballs to a chafing dish. Add barbecue sauce and keep warm over a low flame. Serve with wooden picks. Yield: about 4 dozen.

PARTY MEATBALLS

2 tablespoons butter or margarine	¼ teaspoon pepper
½ cup finely minced onion	1 teaspoon seasoned salt
1½ pounds ground meat (equal parts beef, veal, and pork)	½ teaspoon grated lemon rind
	1 teaspoon lemon juice
2 slices white bread	1 tablespoon Worcestershire sauce
2 eggs	½ teaspoon anchovy paste
3 tablespoons minced fresh parsley or 1 tablespoon dried parsley	About 2 tablespoons salad oil
	3½ cups beef broth (bouillon cubes and hot water may be used)
¼ teaspoon paprika	Sauce

Heat butter in a large skillet or Dutch oven. Add onion and sauté until golden. Put meat in a large bowl. Soak bread in water, squeeze dry, and add to meat. Add onions and all other ingredients except oil and broth. Mix thoroughly, using a wooden spoon or your hands. Form into 1-inch balls and brown in heated oil. Remove to paper towels to drain. Strain drippings from skillet, reserving the brown bits that cling to the skillet if they aren't scorched.

Heat broth in the same skillet and bring to boiling point. Add meatballs, cover, and simmer for 15 minutes. Remove meatballs and prepare Sauce. Place balls in Sauce and heat gently for about 30 minutes. Transfer to a chafing dish just before serving. Yield: 6 to 8 servings.

Sauce:

¼ cup butter or margarine	1 tablespoon drained capers
¼ cup all-purpose flour	1 tablespoon minced parsley
2½ cups meatball liquid	1 teaspoon lemon juice

Heat butter in a large skillet. Blend in flour until smooth and barely golden. Gradually add 2½ cups of the liquid left from cooking the meatballs. Cook, stirring constantly, until smooth. Add capers and parsley, then lemon juice. May be prepared ahead and frozen. Yield: about 2½ cups.

PEANUT BUTTER MEATBALLS

½ cup peanut butter (smooth or crunchy)	2 tablespoons chili sauce
½ pound ground beef	1 teaspoon salt
¼ cup finely chopped onion, or 2 teaspoons instant minced onion	⅛ teaspoon pepper
	1 egg, beaten
	2 tablespoons peanut oil

Combine peanut butter, beef, onion, chili sauce, salt, pepper, and egg; shape into 3 dozen small meatballs. Fry in hot peanut oil, turning to brown on all sides. Serve hot with wooden picks. Yield: 3 dozen.

TANGY-SWEET MEATBALLS

1 pound ground beef	2 teaspoons salt
1 pound ground pork	2 tablespoons margarine
2 cups soft breadcrumbs	1 (10-ounce) jar apricot preserves
2 eggs, slightly beaten	
½ cup finely chopped onion	½ cup barbecue sauce
1 tablespoon minced parsley	

Combine first 7 ingredients, mixing well; shape into 1-inch balls, and brown in margarine. Drain meatballs on paper towels, and place in a 13- x 9- x 2-inch baking dish. Combine preserves and barbecue sauce; mix well, and pour over meatballs. Bake at 350° for 30 minutes. Yield: about 5 dozen.

Photograph for this recipe on page 140

SWEDISH MEATBALLS

3 slices white bread
2 cups water
1½ pounds ground beef
½ pound mild pork sausage
1 onion, minced
3 tablespoons butter or
    margarine, divided

2 medium potatoes, boiled and
    mashed
1 teaspoon salt
⅛ teaspoon pepper
1 teaspoon seasoned salt
2 eggs
Gravy

Soak bread in water for a few minutes; press to drain. Combine beef and sausage with bread. Sauté onion in 1 tablespoon butter; add to meat along with mashed potatoes, seasonings, and eggs. Beat together with electric mixer until light. Shape into 1½-inch balls and brown in remaining butter, gently turning balls to brown evenly; remove carefully. When meatballs are done, prepare Gravy using the same skillet. Return meatballs to skillet. Cover and simmer for 40 minutes. Will freeze. Yield: 10 to 12 servings.

Gravy:

3 tablespoons butter or
    margarine
3 tablespoons all-purpose flour
3 cups beef broth (bouillon
    cubes and water)

1 cup cream
½ teaspoon seasoned salt
1 teaspoon bottled brown
    bouquet sauce
Pepper to taste

Heat butter in same skillet used for browning meatballs; add flour and stir until yellow. Gradually add beef broth and stir until smooth and thick. Add cream and seasoned salt, then bottled brown bouquet sauce and pepper. Yield: about 3 cups.

WATER CHESTNUT MEATBALLS

1 (8½-ounce) can water
    chestnuts, drained and
    chopped
½ pound lean ground beef
½ pound hot sausage

2 cups breadcrumbs
½ cup milk
½ teaspoon onion powder
1 tablespoon soy sauce

Combine all ingredients; shape into 1-inch balls. Bake at 350° for 20 to 30 minutes.

To freeze, place uncooked meatballs about ½ inch apart on a baking sheet (make sure meatballs do not touch each other); cover with aluminum foil, and freeze. After meatballs are thoroughly frozen, remove from baking sheet and store in plastic bags in freezer. Thaw before baking. Yield: about 35 meatballs.

▪ *When making a guest list, include people who have something in common, those you think will be compatible even though they may not know each other well.*

BAKED CREAMY STUFFED MUSHROOMS

18 to 20 medium mushrooms
1 (4½-ounce) can deviled
  ham
1 (3-ounce) package cream
  cheese, softened

2 tablespoons commercial
  sour cream
1 tablespoon minced chives
1 egg yolk, lightly beaten
¼ cup fine breadcrumbs

Clean mushrooms, remove stems, and chop. Place mushroom caps hollow side up on a lightly greased cookie sheet. Combine deviled ham, cream cheese, sour cream, chives, and egg yolk; add chopped mushroom stems and fill caps with mixture. Sprinkle top with breadcrumbs. Bake at 450° for 8 to 10 minutes. Serve immediately. Yield: 20 appetizers.

CHEESE-STUFFED MUSHROOM CAPS

16 to 20 large fresh
  mushrooms
About 5 tablespoons melted
  butter or margarine, divided
½ cup shredded Swiss or
  mozzarella cheese

1 hard-cooked egg, finely
  chopped
3 tablespoons dry
  breadcrumbs

Remove and discard about ¼ inch of mushroom stems. Gently rinse mushrooms, and pat dry. Remove stems; chop and set aside. Brush outside of caps with 3 tablespoons melted butter, and place, cap side down, in a buttered baking dish. Broil 4 inches from heat for 2 minutes; cool to touch.

Combine mushroom stems, cheese, egg, breadcrumbs, and remaining 2 tablespoons melted butter; mix well. Stuff mushroom caps with cheese mixture. Broil 4 inches from heat for 2 minutes. Yield: 8 to 10 servings.

CLAM-STUFFED MUSHROOMS

24 large fresh mushrooms
⅓ cup melted butter or
  margarine
1 (8-ounce) can minced
  clams, drained
3 tablespoons sliced green
  onion

1 tablespoon chopped parsley
¼ teaspoon salt
⅛ teaspoon pepper
⅛ teaspoon garlic powder
¾ cup mayonnaise
½ teaspoon prepared mustard

Clean mushrooms with a damp cloth; remove stems, leaving caps intact. Set mushroom caps aside.

Chop mushroom stems; sauté in butter 10 minutes. Add clams, onion, parsley, salt, pepper, and garlic powder; sauté 5 minutes. Stuff mushroom caps with clam mixture. Place in a lightly greased baking dish; chill.

Combine mayonnaise and mustard; top each mushroom cap with mayonnaise mixture. Bake at 350° for 10 to 15 minutes. Yield: 6 to 8 appetizer servings.

Crab-Stuffed Mushrooms (below)

CRAB-STUFFED MUSHROOMS

12 large or 18 medium
  mushrooms
2 tablespoons salad oil
1 (6-ounce) package frozen
  crabmeat, thawed and
  drained
1 egg, lightly beaten

2 tablespoons mayonnaise
2 tablespoons chopped onion
1 teaspoon lemon juice
½ cup soft breadcrumbs,
  divided
2 tablespoons melted butter or
  margarine

Gently rinse mushrooms, and pat dry. Remove stems. Brush caps with
salad oil, and place in a buttered baking dish.
  Combine crabmeat, egg, mayonnaise, onion, lemon juice, and ¼ cup
breadcrumbs. Stuff caps with crabmeat mixture. Combine remaining ¼
cup breadcrumbs with butter; sprinkle over crab mixture. Bake at 375° for
15 minutes. Yield: 6 servings.
  Note: Mushroom stems may be frozen for use in soups and sauces.

DEVILED CRAB-STUFFED MUSHROOMS

½ cup milk
3 tablespoons butter or
  margarine, divided
15 cheese crackers
1 (6-ounce) package frozen
  crabmeat, thawed and
  coarsely chopped

½ teaspoon dry mustard
1 teaspoon minced onion
½ teaspoon salt
½ teaspoon prepared
  horseradish
Dash of pepper
12 large fresh mushroom caps

Heat milk and 1 tablespoon butter; crumble crackers into milk. Remove from heat. Stir in remaining ingredients except mushroom caps and remaining 2 tablespoons butter. Spoon into mushroom caps. Melt remaining butter and brush mushroom caps. Place in a shallow baking dish. Bake at 350° for 20 to 30 minutes or until mushrooms are tender. Yield: 1 dozen.

MUSHROOMS ROYALE

1 pound medium mushrooms
¼ cup butter or margarine, divided
¼ cup finely chopped green pepper
¼ cup finely chopped onion

1½ cups soft breadcrumbs
½ teaspoon salt
½ teaspoon ground thyme
¼ teaspoon turmeric
¼ teaspoon pepper

Wash, trim, and dry mushrooms thoroughly. Remove stems; finely chop enough stems to measure ⅓ cup. Melt 3 tablespoons butter in a skillet. Cook and stir chopped mushroom stems, green pepper, and onion in butter until tender, about 5 minutes. Remove from heat; stir in remaining ingredients except mushroom caps and remaining 1 tablespoon butter. Melt 1 tablespoon butter in a shallow baking dish. Fill mushroom caps with stuffing mixture; place mushrooms filled side up in butter in a baking dish. Bake at 350° for 15 minutes.

Broil mushrooms 3 to 4 inches from source of heat for 2 minutes. Serve hot. Yield: about 3 dozen.

MUSHROOM-STUFFED ARTICHOKE SHELLS

¼ cup butter or margarine
¼ cup dry white wine
½ teaspoon salt
¼ teaspoon monosodium glutamate
Dash of pepper
30 to 40 (approximately 1 pound) small fresh mushroom caps

10 canned or freshly cooked artichoke shells, including liquid
3 tablespoons water
½ cup commercial sour cream

Melt butter; add wine, salt, monosodium glutamate, and pepper. Add mushroom caps and simmer just until tender, stirring constantly. Steam artichoke shells in their liquid plus the water. Add sour cream to mushroom mixture and heat just until sour cream and sauce are blended. Spoon 3 or 4 mushrooms and sour cream sauce into each artichoke shell. Serve hot as as appetizer. Yield: 10 servings.

MUSHROOMS STUFFED WITH SPINACH SOUFFLÉ

1 (10-ounce) package frozen
   chopped spinach
2 tablespoons butter or
   margarine
2 tablespoons all-purpose flour
½ teaspoon salt

½ cup milk
½ cup grated Parmesan
   cheese
5 eggs, separated
2 to 3 dozen fresh mushroom
   caps, stems removed

Cook spinach according to package directions; drain very thoroughly and set aside. Melt butter over medium heat; add flour, stirring until well mixed. Add salt and milk; stir well. Add spinach. Cook over medium heat until mixture thickens and bubbles. Remove from heat; stir in cheese. Cool. Beat egg yolks until thick and lemon colored; stir yolks into cooled spinach mixture. Beat egg whites until stiff peaks form; carefully fold whites into spinach mixture. Fill mushroom caps with spinach soufflé. Amount of filling used will vary according to size of caps available. Bake at 350° for 15 minutes or until soufflé is puffy. Serve warm. Yield: 2 to 3 dozen.

Note: For hostesses with little time to spare, the frozen prepared spinach soufflé may be substituted for the one made from scratch. If the frozen prepared soufflé is used, it should be thawed before stuffing the mushrooms and baking.

Photograph for this recipe on cover

ANGELS ON HORSEBACK

1 pint select oysters
12 slices bacon, halved
½ teaspoon salt

⅛ teaspoon pepper
⅛ teaspoon paprika
2 tablespoons chopped parsley

Drain oysters and lay each oyster across half a slice of bacon. Sprinkle with seasonings and parsley. Roll bacon around oyster and fasten with a wooden pick. Place oysters on a rack in a shallow baking pan and bake at 450° for about 10 minutes or until bacon is crisp. Remove wooden picks and serve. Yield: 6 servings.

CHAFING DISH OYSTERS

2 (12-ounce) cans oysters,
   undrained
¼ cup butter or margarine
1 (8-ounce) package cream
   cheese, softened
½ cup plus 2 tablespoons dry
   white wine
3 tablespoons chopped
   scallions

½ teaspoon paprika
½ teaspoon anchovy paste
¼ teaspoon cayenne pepper
¼ teaspoon salt
5 or 6 drops hot sauce
Chopped parsley
Individual pastry shells

Place undrained oysters in a saucepan; cook over medium heat about 2 minutes or until edges begin to curl. Drain and set aside.

Combine butter and cream cheese in a medium saucepan; place over low heat, stirring until melted. Add wine, and blend with a wire whisk until smooth. Stir in scallions and seasonings except parsley; bring to a boil over high heat, stirring constantly. Gently fold in oysters.

Spoon oyster mixture into a chafing dish, and keep warm over a low flame. Garnish with parsley, and serve in individual pastry shells. Yield: 20 to 25 appetizers.

Photograph for this recipe on page 6

OYSTER BEIGNETS

1 cup all-purpose flour	1 (7½- or 8-ounce) can
½ teaspoon sugar	oysters, drained and
¼ cup butter or margarine	chopped
1 cup milk	Salad oil
4 eggs	Cocktail Sauce

Combine flour and sugar; set aside. Combine butter and milk in a saucepan; heat over low heat. Add flour mixture and stir vigorously until mixture forms a ball and leaves the sides of the pan; remove from heat. Add eggs, one at a time, beating thoroughly after each addition. Continue beating until a stiff batter is formed. Add oysters to the batter and mix well. Drop mixture by teaspoonfuls into deep hot oil. Fry at 350° for 5 to 6 minutes or until brown. Drain on absorbent paper. Serve with Cocktail Sauce. Yield: about 5 dozen.

Cocktail Sauce:

¾ cup chili sauce	1 tablespoon prepared
¼ cup finely chopped celery	horseradish
1 tablespoon lemon juice	½ teaspoon salt

Combine all ingredients and chill. Yield: about 1 cup.

OYSTER PATTIES

½ pound mushrooms, sliced	Pepper to taste
3 tablespoons melted butter or	1 teaspoon lemon juice
margarine	2 dozen small oysters (about
3 tablespoons all-purpose flour	1 pint), drained
1 cup milk	Baked patty shells
½ teaspoon salt	Parsley (optional)
¼ teaspoon celery salt	

Sauté mushrooms in butter until tender; blend in flour, and cook until bubbly. Gradually add milk; cook until smooth and thickened, stirring constantly. Add salt, celery salt, pepper, lemon juice, and oysters.

Cook over medium-low heat until oysters start to curl up (about 5 minutes); stir occasionally. Serve in patty shells. If desired, garnish with parsley. Yield: 6 to 8 servings.

APPETIZER PIZZA

½ pound ground beef or bulk
   sausage
Butter or margarine
½ teaspoon salt
1 tablespoon instant minced
   onion

4 English muffins
Sauce
⅓ pound mozzarella cheese,
   shredded
1 tablespoon oregano

Sauté meat in 1 teaspoon butter. Add salt and onion; cook until done. Split muffins; spread lightly with butter. Toast under broiler until lightly browned. Spread Sauce over muffin halves. Spoon meat mixture over sauce. Sprinkle with cheese and oregano. Bake at 400° until cheese melts. Cut in quarters and serve. Yield: 8 to 10 servings.

Sauce:

¼ (6-ounce) can tomato paste
¼ cup water

⅓ teaspoon salt
½ teaspoon sugar

Combine all ingredients; blend well. Yield: about ½ cup.

PARTY PIZZAS

2 (10¾-ounce) cans tomato
   soup, undiluted
4 teaspoons oregano
2 teaspoons garlic salt
2 tablespoons Worcestershire
   sauce
½ teaspoon hot pepper sauce

Saltine crackers
Pepperoni, stuffed olives,
   anchovies, chopped onions,
   or mushrooms
Sharp cheese, cut into thin
   slivers

Heat soup in a saucepan; add oregano, garlic salt, Worcestershire sauce, and hot pepper sauce. Cool and keep refrigerated until ready to use.

Put 1 teaspoon soup mixture on each cracker and top with pepperoni, stuffed olives, anchovies, chopped onions, or mushrooms. Place a sliver of cheese over each. Bake at 450° for 5 minutes. Yield: sauce for about 13 dozen pizzas.

PIZZA SANDWICHES

4 English muffins, split
Softened butter or margarine
1 pound mild Italian sausage

1 (8-ounce) can tomato sauce
½ pound Cheddar cheese, cut
   into strips

Toast cut side of muffins; spread with softened butter. Slowly fry sausage until browned and thoroughly cooked; drain on absorbent paper towels. Place muffins on broiler pan; spread each with 1 tablespoon tomato sauce.

Spread muffins with cooked sausage; top with cheese slices, crisscross fashion. Spoon 1 tablespoon tomato sauce over each. Broil until cheese is melted. Yield: 8 small pizzas.

YORKSHIRE PUFFS

1 teaspoon salt	1 pound ground beef
½ cup boiling water	½ teaspoon onion salt
½ cup shortening	½ teaspoon Worcestershire
1 cup all-purpose flour	sauce
4 eggs	Salad oil

Combine salt, boiling water, and shortening; bring to a boil. Add flour all at once, stirring vigorously until ball forms in center of pan. Cool slightly. Add eggs, one at a time, beating well after each addition until mixture is smooth. Mixture should be very stiff.

Brown ground beef. Pour off fat. Add onion salt and Worcestershire sauce to ground beef; add to puff mixture. Heat oil to 365°. Drop puff mixture by teaspoonfuls into hot oil. Deep fry 3 to 5 minutes or until golden brown. Yield: 7 dozen.

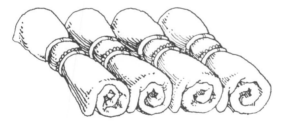

BEEF QUICHE

½ pound ground beef	1¼ cups half-and-half
½ teaspoon salt	¼ teaspoon salt
Pastry for a 9-inch pie shell	Dash of pepper
3 eggs	⅛ teaspoon sugar
6 ounces shredded Swiss	1 teaspoon finely chopped
cheese	chives

Cook ground beef in a heavy skillet until lightly browned, stirring occasionally. Drain well on absorbent paper. Put beef in a mixing bowl; add salt and mix well.

Line a 9-inch piepan with pastry; crimp edges and prick bottom and sides lightly. Beat eggs. Brush pastry with small amount of egg and bake at 450° for 10 minutes. Remove from oven and lower oven temperature to 325°.

Arrange shredded Swiss cheese in bottom of baked shell. Sprinkle ground beef evenly over cheese. To beaten eggs, add half-and-half, salt, pepper, sugar, and chives. Pour egg mixture slowly over beef and cheese. Bake at 325° for 50 minutes. Let stand 10 to 15 minutes before serving. Cut in small wedges to serve as hors d'oeuvres. Yield: 12 servings.

OLIVE QUICHE

6 eggs	2 tablespoons chopped chives
1 cup sliced ripe olives	¾ teaspoon salt
1 (16-ounce) carton	Dash of cayenne pepper
commercial sour cream	Pastry for 2 piecrusts
1 teaspoon oregano	
1½ cups shredded Swiss	
cheese	

Beat eggs with a wooden spoon in a large mixing bowl. Add all ingredients except pastry and mix well. Prepare pastry; roll out to fit a 15- x 10- x 1-inch jelly roll pan, bringing pastry partially up sides of pan. Pour olive mixture over pastry and bake at 425° for 15 minutes. Reduce temperature to 375° and continue baking for about 25 minutes or until filling is set (when a knife inserted in center comes out clean). Cool slightly and cut into bars about 1½ x 2½ inches. Serve warm. Yield: about 4 dozen.

SAUSAGE BALLS

1 pound hot or mild bulk pork	¼ cup catsup
sausage	¼ cup chili sauce
1 egg, slightly beaten	1 tablespoon soy sauce
⅓ cup seasoned breadcrumbs	2 tablespoons brown sugar
(dry packaged herb stuffing)	1 tablespoon vinegar
¼ teaspoon ground sage	½ cup water

Combine first 4 ingredients and mix thoroughly. Shape into balls the size of a quarter. Brown on all sides in a dry skillet; drain on paper towels. Drain fat from skillet; combine catsup, chili sauce, soy sauce, brown sugar, vinegar, and ½ cup water in skillet. Stir well; return meatballs to skillet, cover, and simmer for 30 minutes. Refrigerate or freeze. When ready to serve, reheat, place in a chafing dish, and serve with wooden picks. Yield: about 3 dozen.

SAUSAGE-BACON ROLLUPS

¼ cup butter or margarine	¼ pound hot or mild, bulk
½ cup water	pork sausage
1½ cups packaged	½ to ⅔ pound sliced bacon
herb-seasoned stuffing	Cherry tomatoes
1 egg, slightly beaten	Parsley

Melt butter in water in a saucepan; add to stuffing, mixing well. Add egg and sausage; blend thoroughly. Chill 1 hour for easier handling; then shape into small oblongs, about the size of pecans.

   Cut bacon slices into thirds. Wrap each piece of stuffing mixture with bacon, and fasten with a wooden pick.

   Place on rack in a shallow pan. Bake at 375° for 35 minutes or until brown and crisp, turning at halfway point in cooking. Drain on paper towels and serve hot. Garnish with cherry tomatoes and parsley. Yield: about 3 dozen.

Note: These may be made the day before baking and refrigerated. They may also be frozen before baking. To serve, thaw and bake as directed.

Photograph for this recipe on page 82

SAUSAGE-BISCUIT APPETIZER

1 pound hot pork sausage	½ cup shortening
2⅔ cups all-purpose flour	1 package dry yeast
2 tablespoons sugar	¼ cup very warm water (105°
1 teaspoon baking powder	to 115°)
½ teaspoon soda	1 cup buttermilk
½ teaspoon salt	Melted butter or margarine

Cook sausage very slowly, stirring constantly until done (don't overcook). Drain and set aside. Combine dry ingredients; cut in shortening with a pastry blender.

Dissolve yeast in very warm water; let stand for about 5 minutes. Add to buttermilk. Stir into dry ingredients and mix well. Turn out on a pastry cloth or lightly floured board; roll or pat to about ¼ to ½ inch thick. Brush with melted butter and sprinkle sausage over half the dough. Fold other half of dough over sausage mixture and pat or roll lightly. Cut with a biscuit cutter.

Biscuits may be placed on a cookie sheet and frozen quickly. After they are frozen, they may be placed in moistureproof containers and returned to freezer.

To cook, dip biscuits in melted butter, place on a greased cookie sheet, and bake at 450° for 12 minutes or until brown. Yield: 2 dozen.

SAUSAGE-CHEESE APPETIZERS

1 pound hot sausage, uncooked	3 cups biscuit mix
4 cups shredded mild Cheddar cheese	

Crumble sausage into a large bowl; add cheese and mix well. Blend biscuit mix into sausage and cheese mixture with a pastry blender. Shape into walnut-size balls; place on ungreased cookie sheets. Bake at 350° for 10 to 12 minutes. Yield: about 9 dozen.

Note: After baking, these can be frozen in moistureproof containers. To serve, remove from freezer and heat at 350° until warm.

• *Regardless of the informality of your party, make two time schedules. The first schedule includes any preparation that can be done ahead—preparing some food, checking that linens are in order, polishing silver, or ordering flowers or items that must be rented. The second schedule stipulates timing for all preparation to be done the day of the party. Allow time to relax and get yourself ready at a leisurely pace in time enough to greet early arrivals.*

SAUSAGE BALLS IN CHEESE PASTRY

1 pound hot or mild pork
    sausage
¾ cup dry breadcrumbs
About ⅓ cup chicken broth

⅛ teaspoon ground nutmeg
¼ teaspoon poultry seasoning
Cheese Pastry

Combine all ingredients except Cheese Pastry. Form mixture into small teaspoon-size balls. Fry slowly in a dry skillet until done; drain on paper towels. (If you fry these at low heat, a hard crust should not form.) Make Cheese Pastry.

Cheese Pastry:

1½ cups all-purpose flour
¼ teaspoon salt
1 teaspoon paprika
2 cups shredded Cheddar
    cheese

½ cup butter or margarine,
    softened

Combine flour, salt, and paprika in a large bowl. Stir in Cheddar cheese. Cut in butter; then work with hands until dough is smooth. Pinch off small pieces of dough (about 1 tablespoon) and form smoothly around sausage balls. The balls may be baked at 375° for about 15 to 20 minutes at this point, or placed unbaked in freezer until ready to use. To serve, bake unthawed balls at 400° for about 20 to 25 minutes. Yield: about 4 dozen.

CHEESEAPPLE SAUSAGE SNACKS

2 apples, cored
12 slices party rye bread,
    buttered
2 (5-ounce) cans Vienna
    sausage

1 (10-ounce) round Gouda
    cheese, cut into 12 wedges
Ground cloves

Slice each apple into 6 rings; place an apple ring on each bread slice. Cut 12 sausages in half lengthwise; place two halves cut side down on each apple ring. Broil 2 minutes or until sandwich is hot. Cut 2 remaining sausages crosswise into 6 slices each for garnish. Top sandwiches with a Gouda wedge and sausage slice. Broil 2 to 3 minutes or until cheese is melted. Sprinkle with cloves. Yield: 1 dozen.

MAXINE'S PINWHEELS

2 cups biscuit mix
1 pound ground pork sausage

Chopped chives (optional)

Prepare biscuit mix according to package directions. Roll dough out on a lightly floured surface into a rectangle that measures 15 x 18 inches and about ⅛ inch thick. Dot entire surface with pieces of fresh pork sausage; sprinkle with chives. Cut dough in half crosswise and roll each half, jelly-roll fashion, toward the center, making 2 rolls. Chill for easy slicing (or freeze).

Cut each roll into ½-inch slices. Arrange ½ inch apart in a shallow baking dish. Bake at 450° for 15 minutes or until golden brown. Drain on absorbent paper. Serve hot. Each roll makes about 24 slices. Yield: 4 dozen.

SMOKED SAUSAGE APPETIZERS

3 (20-inch) links sausage   **Justin's Barbecue Sauce**

Place sausage on smoker. Prick sausage with fork while it cooks to allow fat to drain out. Smoke about 20 minutes. Cut sausage in bite-size pieces, and serve with Justin's Barbecue Sauce. Yield: about 6 dozen appetizer servings.

Justin's Barbecue Sauce:

2 medium onions, chopped   **2 tablespoons garlic powder**
¾ cup melted margarine   **2 (26-ounce) bottles catsup**
1½ cups firmly packed dark   **1 (7-ounce) bottle**
** brown sugar**   ** Worcestershire sauce**
1 (24-ounce) jar prepared   **¾ cup lemon juice**
** mustard**   **About 5 cups water**
1 (4-ounce) bottle liquid
** smoke**

Sauté onion in margarine in a large saucepan. Add brown sugar, mixing well. Add remaining ingredients; bring to a boil and simmer over low heat 30 minutes, stirring occasionally. Yield: about 4 quarts.

Note: This sauce stores well in the refrigerator and may be used for chicken, ribs, steaks, or hamburgers.

SMOKY BOBS WITH PIMIENTO AND GHERKIN

1 pound precooked smoked
   sausage
1 cup commercial Italian
   salad dressing
Few drops lemon juice

Dash of garlic salt
1 (4-ounce) jar whole
   pimientos
1 (4-ounce) jar small sweet
   gherkins

Cut sausage into pieces 1 inch thick. Marinate for at least 1 hour in mixture of Italian salad dressing, lemon juice, and garlic salt. Remove sausage from marinade; alternate pieces of sausage with strips of pimiento and sweet gherkins on bamboo skewers. Place on bottom rack of grill; cook at medium heat for 15 minutes. Turn kabobs once during grilling; baste on each side with marinade. Yield: 8 to 10 servings.

Note: For a different taste combination, substitute 1 (3-ounce) jar stuffed green olives and 1 (3½-ounce) jar pitted ripe olives for the pimiento and gherkins.

TUNA PUFFS

2 (6½- or 7-ounce) cans tuna
1 cup finely chopped celery
½ cup mayonnaise or salad
   dressing
2 tablespoons chopped onion

2 tablespoons chopped sweet
   pickle
Salt to taste
Puff Shells

Drain and flake tuna. Combine all ingredients except Puff Shells. Mix thoroughly. Prepare Puff Shells. Cut tops from Puff Shells and fill each shell with approximately 2 teaspoons of salad. Yield: 4½ dozen.

Puff Shells:

½ cup boiling water
¼ cup butter or margarine
Dash of salt

½ cup all-purpose flour
2 eggs

Combine water, butter, and salt; bring to a boil over medium heat. Add flour and stir vigorously until mixture forms a ball and leaves the sides of the pan. Remove from heat. Add eggs, one at a time, beating thoroughly after each addition. Continue beating until a stiff dough is formed. Drop by level teaspoonfuls onto a well-greased cookie sheet. Bake at 450° for 10 minutes. Reduce heat to 350° and continue baking about 10 minutes longer. Yield: 4½ dozen.

SCALLOP KABOBS

½ pound whole, fresh scallops
   (washed)
Stuffed green olives

Pitted black olives
Maraschino cherries

Alternate scallops, green olives, and black olives on bamboo skewers; top each skewer with a cherry. Place on bottom rack of grill; cook at medium heat for 8 to 10 minutes. Yield: 10 to 12 servings.

SKEWERED SCALLOPS

1 pound scallops, fresh or frozen	3 tablespoons honey
1 pint cherry tomatoes	3 tablespoons prepared mustard
2 large green peppers, cut into 1-inch squares	2 tablespoons salad oil
⅓ cup lemon juice	1½ teaspoons curry powder

Thaw frozen scallops and rinse to remove any shell particles. Cut large scallops in half. Alternate scallops, tomatoes, and green peppers on 40 skewers or wooden picks approximately 3 inches long. Place kabobs on a well-greased broiler pan. Combine remaining ingredients. Brush kabobs with sauce. Broil about 4 inches from source of heat for 5 to 7 minutes. Turn carefully and brush with sauce. Broil 5 to 7 minutes longer, basting once. Yield: 3½ dozen.

SESAME SEED STICKS

¾ cup butter or margarine	Ice water
2 cups all-purpose flour	1 cup sesame seed
1 teaspoon salt	Salt
2 dashes of cayenne pepper	

Cut butter into flour mixed with salt and cayenne pepper. Sprinkle ice water over dough and toss with a fork until dough holds together, as for pastry. Roll dough out on a floured board to ⅛-inch thickness and cut into strips 1 x 3 inches. Place on an ungreased cookie sheet, sprinkle generously with sesame seed, and bake at 325° for about 15 minutes. Before removing from pan and while still hot, sprinkle with a little salt. May be frozen. Yield: about 6 dozen.

SHRIMP INEZ

¼ cup butter or margarine	1½ pounds medium raw shrimp, peeled and deveined
1 clove garlic, minced	
½ teaspoon salt	Dash of pepper
1 teaspoon monosodium glutamate	⅓ cup chopped parsley

Melt butter in a large skillet. Add garlic, salt, and monosodium glutamate; sauté until garlic is brown. Add shrimp; sauté, stirring constantly, until shrimp are pink; add pepper and parsley; cook 1 minute longer. Serve in a chafing dish. Yield: about 2½ dozen.

BARBECUED SHRIMP

1 clove garlic, pressed
½ teaspoon salt
½ cup salad oil
¼ cup soy sauce
½ cup lemon juice
3 tablespoons finely chopped
  parsley

2 tablespoons finely chopped
  onion
½ teaspoon pepper
2 pounds large shrimp, peeled

Combine first 8 ingredients to make marinade; mix well. Place shrimp in a shallow dish; add marinade. Cover and refrigerate 2 to 3 hours.

Thread shrimp onto cocktail skewers. Broil or grill over medium heat about 3 to 4 minutes on each side. Serve with cocktail picks. Yield: 15 to 20 appetizer servings.

Photograph for this recipe on page 2

SHRIMP IN JACKETS

¼ cup butter or margarine
1 clove garlic, minced
½ teaspoon onion salt
1 pound shrimp, cooked,
  peeled, and deveined

About 10 slices bacon, cut
  into thirds
Chili sauce
Cheese crackers

Melt butter; stir in garlic and onion salt. Wrap each shrimp in a slice of bacon. Place seam side down on a heavy-duty aluminum foil-lined broiler rack. Broil about 2 minutes on each side or until bacon is crisp, turning once and brushing with butter mixture. Place a small amount of chili sauce on crackers. Top with shrimp. Yield: about 2½ dozen.

LUAU LEIS

1 (13¼-ounce) can pineapple
  chunks
2 tablespoons soy sauce
2 tablespoons lemon juice
1 tablespoon salad oil
1 teaspoon dry mustard

24 shrimp, cooked, peeled,
  and deveined
Macadamia nuts or peanuts,
  finely chopped
Flaked coconut

Drain pineapple and reserve juice. Combine ¼ cup pineapple juice, soy sauce, lemon juice, oil, and mustard. Pour over shrimp; cover and let stand for 30 minutes. Soak 8 bamboo skewers in water. Alternate 3 shrimp and 4 pineapple chunks on each skewer. Brush on remaining marinade. Place on a rack or in a shallow pan. Broil 2 to 3 inches from source of heat, turning and basting until hot and lightly browned, about 3 to 5 minutes. Sprinkle 4 skewers with nuts and 4 with coconut. Yield: 8 servings.

SNAPPY SHRIMP MARINADE

½ cup melted butter or
  margarine
⅓ cup Worcestershire sauce
2 teaspoons garlic puree
1 teaspoon rosemary, finely
  crushed
1 teaspoon cayenne pepper

1 teaspoon salt
1 teaspoon pepper
½ teaspoon celery salt
1 teaspoon olive oil
1½ pounds medium shrimp,
  peeled

Combine all ingredients except shrimp in a saucepan; simmer 10 to 15
minutes. Cool slightly; add shrimp. Cover tightly, and marinate in refrigerator 3 to 8 hours.

Spread shrimp in a single layer in a shallow baking dish; pour marinade
over shrimp. Bake at 400° for 18 to 20 minutes or until done. Yield: 6 to 8
appetizer servings.

SPINACH BALLS

2 (10-ounce) packages frozen
  chopped spinach
3 cups herb-seasoned stuffing
  mix
1 large onion, finely chopped
6 eggs, well beaten
¾ cup melted butter or
  margarine

½ cup grated Parmesan
  cheese
1 tablespoon pepper
1½ teaspoons garlic salt
½ teaspoon thyme

Cook spinach according to package directions; drain well, and squeeze to
remove excess moisture. Combine spinach and remaining ingredients,
mixing well. Shape spinach mixture into ¾-inch balls, and place on lightly
greased cookie sheets. Bake at 325° for 15 to 20 minutes. Yield: 11 dozen.

Note: Spinach Balls can be frozen before baking. Place on cookie sheet,
and freeze until firm. When frozen, remove from cookie sheet and store in
plastic bags. Thaw slightly, and bake at 325° for 20 to 25 minutes.

TERIYAKI

½ cup soy sauce
¼ cup dry white wine
1 tablespoon cider vinegar
1 tablespoon sugar
1 clove garlic, crushed

½ teaspoon ground ginger
1 pound top round, cut into
  thin slices about 2 inches
  long
Crackers

Combine soy sauce, wine, vinegar, sugar, garlic, and ginger. Pour over
sliced meat. Cover and marinate for several hours at room temperature or
in the refrigerator overnight. Broil for 5 to 7 minutes, turning once. Place
in a chafing dish and serve with crackers. Yield: about 18 servings.

STEAK BITS

1 (3¾-pound) 2-inch-thick sirloin steak	2 tablespoons dry mustard
Unseasoned instant meat tenderizer	2 teaspoons Worcestershire sauce
1 cup dry red wine or beer	1 teaspoon garlic salt
1 clove garlic, pressed	6 to 8 drops hot sauce
1 cup melted butter or margarine	Dash of pepper

Sprinkle steak with tenderizer, and pierce with fork; place steak in a shallow baking dish. Combine wine and garlic; pour over steak. Cover; marinate in refrigerator 1 hour, turning once.

Remove steak from marinade; reserve ¼ cup marinade. Broil steak 3 to 4 inches from heat 10 to 15 minutes; turn steak, and broil 10 to 15 minutes, depending on desired degree of doneness. Cut steak into bite-size strips; transfer to a chafing dish to keep warm.

Combine ¼ cup reserved marinade and remaining ingredients in a saucepan; stir well. Cook sauce over low heat 5 minutes. Pour sauce over steak or serve sauce separately. Yield: about 12 to 16 appetizer servings.

TUNA TEASERS

1 cup all-purpose flour	1 (6½-ounce) can tuna, drained and flaked
1½ teaspoons baking powder	1 cup shredded process American cheese
1 teaspoon onion salt	1 tablespoon minced green pepper
½ teaspoon curry powder	
Dash of cayenne pepper	
¼ cup butter or margarine	
½ cup milk	

Combine flour, baking powder, onion salt, curry powder, and cayenne pepper; cut in butter with pastry blender or a fork until mixture resembles coarse meal. Add milk and stir until well blended. Add tuna, cheese, and green pepper; blend well.

Drop from a teaspoon onto a greased cookie sheet. Bake at 450° for 10 to 15 minutes or until golden brown. Serve warm. Yield: 3 dozen.

HOT COCKTAIL TURNOVERS

Cream Cheese Pastry	Salt and pepper to taste
½ small onion, minced	2 tablespoons dillweed
3 to 4 tablespoons melted butter or margarine	1 to 2 teaspoons beef bouillon (optional)
½ pound lean ground beef	½ cup hot cooked rice
1 egg, slightly beaten and divided	

Prepare Cream Cheese Pastry according to directions below. Sauté onion in butter for 1 minute. Add beef and half of the beaten egg; cook until beef is done, stirring well. Add salt, pepper, and dillweed. If mixture looks dry, add 1 to 2 teaspoons beef bouillon. Combine meat mixture with rice. Put approximately 1½ teaspoons filling in center of each pastry round. Fold round in half to make a crescent shape. Seal edges together with tines of fork. Brush each crescent with remaining half of egg. Bake at 400° for 10 minutes or until golden brown. Yield: about 2½ dozen.

Cream Cheese Pastry:

1 cup all-purpose flour
½ cup butter or margarine, softened

½ (8-ounce) package cream cheese, softened

Work all ingredients together in a bowl; pat into a ball. Wrap in waxed paper and chill for several hours. Roll out pastry very thin and cut into 2-inch rounds with cutter. Yield: 2½ dozen.

Note: If you wish to freeze the turnovers, you may partially bake them and save the final browning until they are removed from the freezer for serving. Any favorite meat filling can be used with this pastry. It's a good way to use up leftover meat. If leftover meat is used, it will require less cooking time for the filling—just be sure the filling ingredients are tossed together in the pan long enough for the egg to be cooked.

Photograph for this recipe on cover

FRIED WONTONS

1 pound ground pork
2 green onions, finely chopped
1 (8½-ounce) can water chestnuts, drained and finely chopped
1 stalk celery, finely chopped
2 eggs, beaten
1 tablespoon soy sauce

1 teaspoon salt
½ teaspoon pepper
1 (16-ounce) package wonton skins
Salad oil
Commercial sweet-and-sour sauce (optional)

Combine pork, green onion, water chestnuts, celery, eggs, soy sauce, salt, and pepper in a large bowl; mix well.

Separate only a few wonton skins at a time; they dry out quickly. Place 1 teaspoon meat mixture in center of each wonton skin. Moisten edges of each skin with water; fold in half diagonally over filling to form a triangle, pressing edges to seal. Moisten center point, and fold down like an envelope. Moisten two outer points; fold toward center, overlapping slightly; press lightly to seal.

Heat 2 inches of salad oil to 375° in an electric skillet. Add wontons, and fry until golden brown on both sides (about 2 minutes per side). Drain well on paper towels. Serve hot with sweet-and-sour sauce, if desired.

Fried wontons may be frozen and reheated; bake at 325° for 15 to 20 minutes. Yield: 40 to 50.

Note: To make wonton soup, drop about 1 dozen uncooked wontons into 1 quart boiling chicken broth; return to a boil, and cook 5 minutes. Remove from heat, and stir in 1 well-beaten egg white. Top with chopped green onions before serving. Yield: 4 servings.

Marinated Artichoke Hearts (page 60); Marinated Baby Carrots (page 62); Caper-Stuffed Eggs (page 67); Marinated Mushrooms (page 69)

cold appetizers

Pull up a chair, relax on your deck, and reach for something to nibble on. This assortment of cold appetizers offers a variety of tempters before dinner and several together could even be a meal in itself.

Tempting appetizers that you can prepare ahead give you a head start on any party. That's just what makes this selection of snacks so appealing; all are quick and easy to prepare and can be whipped up early in the day.

With this assortment of snacks, your party will get off to a good start and be a memorable, festive occasion, too.

CHILI ALMONDS

2 tablespoons butter or margarine	1 large clove garlic, crushed
1 tablespoon chili powder	2 cups unblanched almonds
	Coarse salt

Put butter in a shallow pan in a 250° oven. When melted, stir in chili powder and garlic. Add almonds and stir until all are coated. Return to oven and bake for about 1½ hours, stirring every 15 minutes or so if convenient. While still hot, sprinkle generously with salt and when cool, store in an airtight container. May be made weeks ahead of time and frozen. Yield: 10 servings.

PARTY ALMONDS

For each cup of almonds, use 1 teaspoon butter or salad oil. Put butter in a shallow pan in a 300° oven; when melted, stir in almonds and bake for 20 to 25 minutes, stirring frequently. Remove and toss with garlic salt and a little cayenne pepper. These keep well in an airtight container. Prepare 2 cups to serve 6.

MARINATED ANCHOVIES

3 (2-ounce) cans rolled anchovies, undrained	6 tablespoons minced fresh parsley
1 clove garlic, crushed	Rye bread
¼ cup wine vinegar	
1 large onion, very finely minced	

Arrange anchovies and some of their liquid in a shallow serving dish. Combine garlic and vinegar and pour over anchovies. Mix onion and parsley; spread in a thick layer over anchovies. Carefully spoon marinade in dish over all to moisten; cover and refrigerate for at least 3 hours. Serve with small rounds of rye bread. Yield: 10 servings.

PARTY ANTIPASTO TRAY

½ medium head iceberg lettuce	1 (2-ounce) can anchovies with capers, drained
1 small head endive	8 ounces provolone cheese, cubed
1 (3½-ounce) package thinly sliced pepperoni	1 (8-ounce) jar peperoncini, drained
1 (4-ounce) package thinly sliced Genoa salami, quartered	1 pound cherry tomatoes
	Radishes
1 (3-ounce) package thinly sliced Italian ham	Carrot sticks
	Ripe olives
1 (15-ounce) can garbanzo beans, drained	Green olives
	Dressing

Party Antipasto Tray (page 58)

Shred lettuce and part of endive. Combine shredded salad greens; toss well and spread over bottom of serving tray.

Make a border of remaining endive leaves around edge of tray. Arrange meats, vegetables, and cubed cheese on top of shredded salad greens. Serve with Dressing. Yield: about 10 to 12 servings.

Dressing:

2 tablespoons water
¼ cup wine vinegar
1 cup salad oil
1 tablespoon olive oil
1 clove garlic, crushed

1 teaspoon ground oregano
1 teaspoon basil
¼ teaspoon thyme
Salt and pepper to taste
 (optional)

Combine all ingredients; mix well. Let stand several hours at room temperature. Yield: about 1½ cups.

ARTICHOKE BALLS

2 cloves garlic, pressed	¾ cup grated Parmesan
2 tablespoons olive oil	cheese, divided
2 (8½-ounce) cans artichoke	¾ cup Italian-seasoned
hearts, drained and mashed	breadcrumbs, divided
2 eggs, slightly beaten	

Sauté garlic in oil about 2 minutes. Add artichokes and eggs; cook, stirring constantly, over low heat 5 minutes.

Remove from heat; stir in ½ cup cheese and ½ cup breadcrumbs. Roll into 1-inch balls. Combine remaining cheese and breadcrumbs; roll balls in mixture. Chill until firm. Yield: about 3½ dozen.

ITALIAN ARTICHOKE HEARTS

1 (16-ounce) can artichoke	¼ cup mayonnaise
hearts, drained	2 tablespoons drained capers
3 tablespoons commercial	Paprika
Italian or French salad	
dressing	

Drain artichoke hearts and cut into halves. Place in a shallow dish, cut side up. Blend dressing and mayonnaise; stir in capers. Spoon over artichoke hearts and chill for several hours. Before serving, sprinkle with paprika and, if desired, scatter a few more drained capers over all. Serve with wooden picks. Yield: 6 servings.

MARINATED ARTICHOKE HEARTS

½ cup vinegar	¼ teaspoon salt
½ cup salad oil	1 (16-ounce) can artichoke
1 small clove garlic, crushed	hearts, drained
1 teaspoon seasoned salt	Minced fresh parsley

Combine all ingredients except artichokes and parsley in saucepan; bring to boil. Split artichokes and add to mixture. Bring mixture to boil; cover and simmer for 10 minutes. Add parsley.

Refrigerate artichokes overnight in a covered dish or jar. Drain well before serving. Yield: 6 servings.

Photograph for this recipe on page 56

ASPARAGUS SPEARS ROLLED IN HAM

18 canned asparagus spears	Pepper
¾ cup salad oil	½ teaspoon basil
¼ cup wine vinegar	9 thin slices boiled or baked
½ teaspoon salt	ham

Marinate asparagus in salad oil, vinegar, salt, pepper, and basil for 2 hours. Drain thoroughly. Cut ham in half crosswise and wrap around asparagus spears, securing each with a wooden pick. Yield: 6 servings.

BACON-AND-RYE BALLS

1 pound bacon	2 teaspoons finely chopped
1 (8-ounce) package cream	onion
cheese, softened	1 teaspoon Worcestershire
¼ cup evaporated milk	sauce
1 cup fine rye breadcrumbs	¾ to 1 cup chopped parsley

Cook bacon until crisp; drain and crumble. Combine bacon, cream cheese, milk, breadcrumbs, onion, and Worcestershire; mix well. Chill 2 hours, and shape into 1-inch balls; roll each in parsley. Yield: about 2 dozen.

Photograph for this recipe on page 134

RIBBON BOLOGNA WEDGES

1 (5-ounce) jar cream cheese	¼ cup finely chopped nuts
with olives and pimiento	Parsley flakes or chopped
12 thin slices bologna	fresh parsley

Have cheese at room temperature. Spread evenly over bologna and sprinkle each piece with chopped nuts. Divide bologna into 2 stacks of 6 slices. Garnish tops with parsley.

Cover both rolls with plastic wrap and chill. At serving time, cut each stack into 16 wedges and insert a colored wooden pick in each wedge. Yield: 32 appetizers.

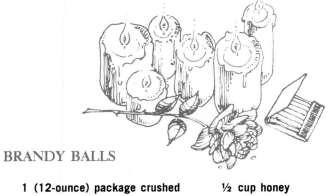

BRANDY BALLS

1 (12-ounce) package crushed	½ cup honey
vanilla wafers	1 pound ground walnuts
½ cup light rum	Powdered sugar
½ cup brandy	

Mix wafers, rum, brandy, honey, and walnuts. Shape into small balls and roll in powdered sugar; store in a tightly-covered container in the refrigerator. These will keep for 5 weeks in the refrigerator. Yield: about 4 dozen.

BRAZIL NUT CHIPS

1½ cups shelled Brazil nuts
2 tablespoons butter or
   margarine

1 teaspoon salt

Prepare nuts for shelling by placing in a saucepan and covering with cold water. Bring to a boil and cook uncovered for 3 minutes. Drain. Again cover with cold water and let stand for 1 minute. Drain. The nuts will crack with greater ease and kernels will remain whole and crunchy.

Cover shelled whole Brazil nuts with cold water. Bring slowly to a boil; then simmer 2 or 3 minutes. Drain and cut lengthwise into thin slices about ⅛ inch thick. (A vegetable peeler or bean-cutting device is helpful.) Spread slices thinly on a shallow buttered pan. Dot with butter; sprinkle with salt. Bake at 350° for about 12 minutes. Stir two or three times. Watch carefully; they burn easily.

Stored in a well-covered container in the refrigerator, Brazil Nut Chips keep fresh for many weeks. They are best if warmed and crisped briefly before serving. Yield: 1½ cups.

MARINATED BROCCOLI

2 bunches fresh broccoli
¼ cup olive oil
1 teaspoon garlic salt

½ cup sliced stuffed green
   olives
¼ cup lemon juice

Rinse broccoli and dry thoroughly. Cut off flowerets in bite-size pieces. Toss flowerets in olive oil to wet them until they glisten; sprinkle with garlic salt and toss again. Sprinkle olives over broccoli. Add lemon juice to mixture and toss to mix thoroughly. Cover and refrigerate for several hours, tossing occasionally. Serve chilled. Yield: 12 to 15 servings.

Photograph for this recipe on cover

MARINATED BABY CARROTS

8 small carrots
3 tablespoons vinegar
3 tablespoons salad oil
1 small clove garlic, crushed

¾ teaspoon seasoned salt
¼ teaspoon salt
Minced fresh parsley

Peel and cut carrots into short, 3-inch sticks. Place in shallow dish; combine other ingredients except parsley and pour over carrots, spooning marinade over carrots so all will be coated. Cover tightly and refrigerate overnight, turning carrots occasionally. Drain off marinade; sprinkle carrots with parsley. Yield: 6 to 8 servings.

Photograph for this recipe on page 56

CHICKEN-STUFFED CELERY

1 (3-ounce) package cream
   cheese, softened
1 (4¾-ounce) can chicken
   spread

½ teaspoon mild curry powder
24 (1½- to 2-inch) celery
   slices
Paprika

Combine cream cheese, chicken spread, and curry. Stuff celery slices. Sprinkle with paprika. Chill. Serve cold. Yield: 2 dozen.

NUTTY STUFFED CELERY

1 bunch celery	¼ cup finely chopped pecans
1 (4½-ounce) can deviled ham	2 tablespoons commercial sour cream
1 tablespoon lemon juice	

Separate celery into stalks; trim, and wash thoroughly. Cut stalks into 3-inch pieces.

Combine remaining ingredients, mixing until smooth. Spread mixture on each piece of celery. Chill. Yield: about 12 servings.

Photograph for this recipe on page 144

SHRIMP-STUFFED CELERY

1 (4½-ounce) can shrimp, drained and chopped	1½ teaspoons finely chopped onion
⅓ cup mayonnaise	1 tablespoon chopped walnuts
¼ cup crushed pineapple	¼ teaspoon salt
2 teaspoons minced parsley	Dash of hot pepper sauce
1½ teaspoons lemon juice	2- to 3-inch celery sticks

Combine first 9 ingredients, mixing well; stuff mixture into celery sticks. Yield: 8 servings.

STUFFED CELERY DIABLE

4 to 5 stalks celery	Pinch of cayenne pepper
2 ounces Roquefort or blue cheese	¼ cup finely ground walnuts
1 (3-ounce) package cream cheese, softened	Paprika

Peel and cut celery into 4-inch pieces. Combine Roquefort and cream cheese until smooth in small bowl of electric mixer. Beat in cayenne pepper; then stir in walnuts. Stuff celery; sprinkle with paprika. Yield: 4 servings.

• *If you're hosting a party without help, ask a friend to help replenish trays as needed. Most guests are pleased to assist.*

• *Plan only one or two party foods that will need attention immediately before serving. Instead, concentrate on dishes that can be prepared ahead.*

• *Note how many items are to be baked, and make sure you'll have adequate oven space. Make use of electric skillets, toaster ovens, and warming trays for additional heating space.*

PARTY CHEESIES

1 egg white, slightly beaten
1 teaspoon water
1½ cups shredded Swiss cheese
¼ cup grated Parmesan cheese
½ cup margarine, softened
¾ cup all-purpose flour
¾ teaspoon salt
⅛ teaspoon ground nutmeg
Paprika

Combine egg white and water, beating lightly with a fork; set aside.

Combine cheese and margarine, mixing well. Add flour, salt, and nutmeg; stir with a fork until a stiff dough is formed. Wrap in aluminum foil, and chill for 15 minutes.

Shape dough into ¾-inch balls, and place on a greased baking sheet. Flatten each with a fork, and brush with egg white mixture.

Bake at 425° for 10 minutes or just until edges begin to brown. Allow to cool, and sprinkle lightly with paprika. Yield: about 4 dozen.

DUO CHEESE BALLS

1 (3-ounce) package blue cheese
2 (3-ounce) packages cream cheese
¼ teaspoon hot pepper sauce
2 teaspoons grated onion
¼ cup finely minced parsley

Have cheese at room temperature. Combine all ingredients. Shape into small balls. Chill well. Serve on wooden picks. Yield: 3 dozen.

ZIPPY CHEESE BALL APPETIZERS

2 (3-ounce) packages cream cheese, softened
1 tablespoon prepared horseradish
1 teaspoon milk (optional)
¼ cup finely chopped dried beef
½ cup crushed potato chips
½ cup finely chopped fresh parsley

Blend cream cheese and horseradish until smooth. (If mixture is a bit stiff, add 1 teaspoon milk.) Add dried beef and potato chips and combine thoroughly. Chill mixture until cream becomes stiff. Shape into 24 to 26 small balls. Roll in parsley and serve on wooden picks. Yield: about 2 dozen.

BUTTERCUP CHEESE STRAWS

3½ cups all-purpose flour
¼ teaspoon salt
¾ teaspoon cayenne pepper
¾ pound butter or margarine, softened
4 cups shredded sharp Cheddar cheese

Combine flour, salt, and cayenne in a large bowl. Cut butter into small pieces, and blend into dry ingredients with fingers until mixture resembles coarse crumbs.

Add cheese, and continue blending until dough is no longer crumbly.

Work with a fourth of the dough at a time. Roll out each piece into a rectangle ⅓ inch thick. Using a pastry wheel, cut dough into strips ½ inch wide and about 4 inches long.

Place strips on ungreased cookie sheets, and bake at 375° for 10 to 12 minutes or until very lightly browned. Do not overbake. Cool. Store in an airtight container, placing waxed paper between layers. These freeze well. Yield: about 10½ dozen.

Photograph for this recipe on page 82

SNAPPY CHEESE WAFERS

2 cups shredded sharp Cheddar cheese	½ teaspoon dry mustard
1 cup butter or margarine, softened	1 cup all-purpose flour
¼ to ½ teaspoon red pepper	1 cup self-rising flour
	2 cups crisp rice cereal

Combine cheese and margarine; cream until smooth, using electric mixer. Add pepper, mustard, and flour; mix well. Stir in rice cereal.

Form dough into small balls; flatten with a fork to make wafers. Place on lightly greased cookie sheets. Bake at 350° for 12 to 15 minutes or until lightly brown. Store in airtight container. Yield: about 3 dozen.

Photograph for this recipe on page 134

ROQUEFORT COCKTAIL BALLS

¼ pound Roquefort cheese	½ cup commercial sour cream
1 tablespoon chopped celery	Paprika
1 tablespoon chopped scallion or green onion	

In a blender or with a fork, blend Roquefort cheese, celery, scallion, and sour cream. Shape into small balls the size of a walnut; sprinkle with paprika. Chill. Yield: about 2 dozen.

PECAN ROQUEFORT HORS D'OEUVRES

½ pound Roquefort cheese	Dash of Worcestershire sauce
¼ cup butter or margarine	Dash of salt and pepper
1 teaspoon grated onion	48 pecan halves
⅛ cup minced celery	

Mash Roquefort cheese. Add butter, onion, celery, and Worcestershire sauce. Beat until smooth and well blended. Add salt and pepper to taste. Chill.

With moistened hands, roll mixture into small balls. Press 2 pecan halves on either side of each cheese ball. Serve at once. Yield: 2 dozen.

LOMI LOMI CHERRIES

1 quart cherry tomatoes
¼ pound smoked salmon,
  minced

1 onion, minced
1 green pepper, minced

Cut off and discard tops of cherry tomatoes. Scoop out seed and pulp with a small pointed spoon. Combine pulp with minced salmon, onion, and green pepper. Refill tomatoes with this mixture and chill before serving. Yield: 2 to 3 dozen.

CHICKEN SALAD BALLS

1 cup chopped cooked
  chicken
1 tablespoon chopped onion
2 tablespoons chopped
  pimiento

Dash of hot sauce
½ cup salad dressing or
  mayonnaise
1 cup chopped pecans

Combine all ingredients, mixing well. Chill 3 to 4 hours, and shape into 1-inch balls. Yield: about 2 dozen.

ORANGE CHICKEN FLUFFS

2 (4¾-ounce) cans chicken
  spread
2 tablespoons chopped toasted
  almonds
¾ cup chopped mandarin
  oranges

½ cup whipping cream,
  whipped
15 to 20 medium cream puff
  shells or 30 to 40 small
  shells
Mandarin orange slices

Combine chicken spread, almonds, and chopped oranges; fold in whipped cream. Chill. Fill puff shells with mixture. Garnish top of each with a mandarin orange slice. Yield: 15 to 20 servings.

COCKTAIL CRUNCH

½ cup butter or margarine
1 (6-ounce) package blue
  cheese or garlic salad
  dressing mix
1 tablespoon Worcestershire
  sauce

1 teaspoon seasoned salt
4 cups bite-size shredded
  wheat cereal
2 cups bite-size rice cereal
2 cups unblanched whole
  almonds

Melt butter in a large shallow pan in a 250° oven. Stir in cheese, Worcestershire sauce, and seasoned salt. Add cereals and almonds; stir well until all are coated. Return to oven and bake for 1 hour, stirring every 15 minutes. May be prepared the day before; also freezes well. Yield: about 8½ cups.

DEVILED EGGS WITH SALTED ALMONDS

12 hard-cooked eggs
¼ cup mayonnaise
¼ cup commercial sour cream
1 teaspoon salt
1 tablespoon Dijon mustard

Dash of cayenne pepper
(optional)
⅓ cup chopped salted
almonds

Cut eggs in half and scoop out yolks. Mash yolks with mayonnaise and sour cream; add salt and mustard and blend well. Taste and add more seasonings if mixture is too bland. (You may want to add a dash of cayenne pepper.) Refill egg whites and sprinkle with chopped almonds. Yield: 1 dozen.

ANCHOVY-STUFFED EGGS

2 hard-cooked eggs
¼ cup butter or margarine,
softened

8 anchovy fillets, mashed
1 tablespoon capers
Pimiento strips

Cut eggs in half lengthwise and remove yolks. In small bowl, mix yolks, butter, anchovy, and capers until well blended. Stuff egg whites with mixture. Garnish each half with a pimiento strip. Yield: 2 servings.

CAPER-STUFFED EGGS

4 hard-cooked eggs
3 anchovy fillets, drained and
liquid reserved, or 2
teaspoons anchovy paste
1 tablespoon drained capers
4 ripe olives, pitted

2 tablespoons mayonnaise
½ teaspoon anchovy liquid
Pepper to taste
About 2 teaspoons lemon juice
Paprika

Cut eggs in half; put yolks through a fine sieve. Grind anchovies, capers, and olives in a food grinder or chop finely in a wooden bowl. Combine with mayonnaise and sieved yolks. Add anchovy liquid, pepper, and about 2 teaspoons lemon juice. Fill whites and sprinkle with paprika. Yield: 8 halves.

Photograph for this recipe on page 56

HAM-STUFFED EGGS

2 hard-cooked eggs
1 tablespoon commercial sour
cream
2 tablespoons minced green
onion

2 slices boiled ham, finely
chopped
½ teaspoon prepared mustard
Salt and pepper to taste

Cut eggs in half lengthwise and remove yolks. Mix yolks and remaining ingredients except whites until well blended. Stuff whites with mixture. Yield: 2 servings.

KASPIN STUFFED EGGS

1 (10½-ounce) can beef
   consommé, undiluted
2 dozen hard-cooked egg
   whites, halved

1 tablespoon curry powder
½ cup mayonnaise
1 (2-ounce) jar red caviar
Parsley sprigs

Refrigerate consommé overnight to congeal. Put approximately 1½ teaspoons consommé in each egg white. Combine curry powder and mayonnaise. Put a dollop of curry mayonnaise on top of consommé in each egg white. Place a small amount of red caviar on top of curry mayonnaise as a garnish. Garnish serving platter with sprigs of parsley. Yield: 4 dozen.

Photograph for this recipe on cover

LOBSTER-STUFFED EGGS

1 pound cooked lobster meat
⅔ cup mayonnaise or salad
   dressing
1 tablespoon chili sauce
1 teaspoon grated onion

1 teaspoon chopped green
   pepper
1 teaspoon chopped pimiento
1½ dozen hard-cooked eggs
Parsley

Chop lobster meat. Add mayonnaise, chili sauce, onion, green pepper, and pimiento. Chill. Cut eggs in half lengthwise and remove yolks. Place lobster mixture in egg whites. Garnish with parsley. Yield: 3 dozen.

SAVORY STUFFED EGGS

8 hard-cooked eggs
6 tablespoons mayonnaise
¼ teaspoon curry powder
¼ cup minced celery
¼ teaspoon salt

1 (4¾-ounce) can chicken
   spread
Salt and pepper
Paprika

Halve eggs lengthwise; carefully remove yolks. Mash only 4 of the yolks and combine with remaining ingredients (except seasonings). Generously refill eggs. Sprinkle with salt and pepper. Cover and chill. Garnish with paprika. Yield: 16 appetizers.

FROZEN FRUIT CUP

1 cup fruit cocktail or fruit cut
   into pieces
½ cup seedless grapes
½ cup watermelon balls

1 (32-ounce) bottle ginger ale,
   chilled
Mint leaves

Combine fruits; place in an ice cube tray. Pour ginger ale over fruit and freeze 1½ to 2 hours or until mixture is a mush. Serve in sherbet glasses; garnish with mint leaves. Yield: 8 servings.

HAM AND CHEESE CURLS

1 (4½-ounce) can deviled
 ham
1 teaspoon lemon juice
1 tablespoon minced green
 onion

¼ cup cracker crumbs
5 slices mozzarella cheese
Paprika

Combine deviled ham, lemon juice, onion, and cracker crumbs; spread on cheese slices and roll. Coat with paprika; wrap in waxed paper and chill. Slice and serve. Yield: 4 dozen.

SNAPPY HAM AND EGG ROLLS

1 (4½-ounce) can deviled
 ham
2 hard-cooked eggs, chopped
1 teaspoon prepared mustard

½ cup crushed potato chips
Sour Cream Sauce

Combine deviled ham, eggs, and mustard; chill. Shape into small balls and chill well. Just before serving, roll balls in crushed potato chips. Serve on wooden picks to dunk in Sour Cream Sauce. Yield: about 2 dozen.

Sour Cream Sauce:

½ cup commercial sour cream
¼ cup catsup

½ teaspoon seasoned salt

Combine all ingredients; chill. Yield: about ¾ cup.

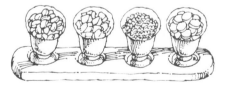

MARINATED MUSHROOMS

1 pound small fresh
 mushrooms
½ teaspoon salt
¼ teaspoon freshly ground
 black pepper

1 teaspoon oregano
⅓ cup wine vinegar
1 cup olive oil or salad oil

Wipe mushrooms with a damp cloth; trim stem end of mushrooms. Mix remaining ingredients; add to mushrooms, and toss until mushrooms are well coated with the marinade. Let stand at room temperature for at least 4 hours. Yield: about 4 cups.

Photograph for this recipe on page 56

PICKLED MUSHROOMS

1 pound fresh mushrooms, or 2 (4-ounce) cans button mushrooms, drained	1 teaspoon salt
½ cup vinegar	1 clove garlic, minced
½ cup salad oil	1 tablespoon chopped chives
	1 bay leaf

Wash fresh mushrooms quickly in cold water and cut off thin slice from bottom of stems. Combine remaining ingredients and pour over mushrooms. Cover and marinate at least overnight, turning several times. Yield: about 12 servings.

SWEDISH NUTS

1 cup whole blanched almonds	1 cup sugar
½ cup butter or margarine	Dash of salt
2 egg whites	1 cup walnut halves
	1 cup pecan halves

Spread almonds on a cookie sheet. Roast at 325° until lightly browned, about 15 to 20 minutes, stirring occasionally; cool. Melt butter in oven in a 13- x 9- x 2-inch baking pan.

Beat egg whites until stiff; add sugar and salt, and continue beating until very stiff. Fold in almonds, walnuts, and pecans; spread nut mixture in baking pan over melted butter.

Bake at 325° about 30 minutes or until mixture is browned and all butter is absorbed, stirring and turning every 10 minutes to cook evenly. Yield: about 4 cups.

PICKLED OKRA

Garlic (1 clove for each jar)	1 quart white vinegar
Hot pepper (1 for each jar)	1 cup water
Okra	½ cup salt
Dillseed (1 teaspoon for each jar)	

Place garlic and hot pepper in the bottom of sterilized, hot pint jars. Pack firmly with clean, young okra pods from which only part of the stem has been removed. Stem end must be open. Add dillseed.

After packing jars, bring vinegar, water, and salt to a boil. Simmer about 5 minutes and pour, while boiling hot, over okra. Seal jars immediately. Yield: 5 to 7 pints.

DILLED GREEN OLIVES

1 (8-ounce) jar unstuffed
  jumbo green olives
1 clove garlic, split
1 small whole dried red
  pepper*
1 teaspoon dillseed

¼ teaspoon pepper
⅔ cup salad oil
⅓ cup cider vinegar

Drain olives and put in jar with tight lid. Add all other ingredients. Prepare several days ahead of serving and keep refrigerated, turning jar upside down several times to distribute the marinade. Yield: about 1½ cups.
  *Use one from your mixed pickling spices.

GARLIC OLIVES

2 (8-ounce) jars green or
  black olives
⅓ cup olive oil

1 tablespoon minced garlic
½ teaspoon oregano

Drain olives, reserving ½ cup liquid. Combine liquid with olive oil, garlic, and oregano. Pack olives into jars; cover with marinade and refrigerate at least 24 hours before serving. Yield: 2 cups.

MARINATED SPANISH OLIVES

1 (8-ounce) jar unpitted green
  olives
¼ cup vinegar
¼ cup olive oil

2 tablespoons minced chives
1 clove garlic, slashed
¼ teaspoon whole
  peppercorns

Drain olives; then add remaining ingredients to them. Fasten lid tightly on jar and let olives stand for 24 hours at room temperature, turning the jar upside down occasionally to distribute the marinade. Yield: 1 cup.

SPICED RIPE OLIVES

1 (16-ounce) jar ripe olives
1 small dried chili pepper*
2 cloves crushed garlic

Few sprigs fresh dill, or about
  ½ teaspoon dillweed
3 tablespoons olive oil

Drain olives, reserving liquid. Add other ingredients to jar; then fill jar with reserved liquid. Let olives marinate 2 days before serving. Yield: 2 cups.
  *Use one from your mixed pickling spices.

CURRIED ALMOND-STUFFED OLIVES

¾ cup toasted slivered
almonds, finely chopped
¼ teaspoon tarragon
½ teaspoon paprika
1 teaspoon curry powder
¼ teaspoon seasoned pepper
½ teaspoon salt

2 teaspoons parsley flakes
½ (8-ounce) package cream
cheese, softened
2 tablespoons whipping cream
2 (7-ounce) cans pitted jumbo
green or ripe olives,
drained

Combine almonds, tarragon, paprika, curry powder, seasoned pepper, salt, and parsley. Combine cream cheese and whipping cream; blend into almond mixture. Split each olive lengthwise. Put the olive halves together with cheese stuffing. Chill for several hours. Yield: about 4 dozen.

MEXICAN STUFFED OLIVES

1 (7¼-ounce) can pitted ripe
olives
4 teaspoons diced anchovy
fillets
⅓ cup wine vinegar

1 tablespoon olive oil
¼ cup chopped pimiento
1 clove garlic, minced
¼ cup chopped parsley

Drain olives; stuff with anchovies. Combine vinegar, olive oil, pimiento, and garlic; pour over olives. Cover and chill for 6 hours or overnight, spooning marinade over olives occasionally. Add parsley. Yield: 2 cups.

PARTY MIX

½ cup butter or margarine
1 (1⅜-ounce) package dry
onion soup mix
1 (7½-ounce) box cheese
crackers

3 to 4 cups bite-size shredded
rice cereal

Put butter in a 12- x 8- x 2-inch pan in a 250° oven. When melted, stir in dry onion soup mix and blend thoroughly. Add other ingredients; stir well to coat thoroughly and bake for about 1 hour, stirring 3 or 4 times. Will freeze. Yield: about 8 cups.

BARBECUE PEANUTS

1 tablespoon liquid smoke
1 teaspoon Worcestershire
sauce
⅓ cup water

1½ cups salted peanuts
1 tablespoon melted butter or
margarine
¼ teaspoon garlic salt

Combine liquid smoke, Worcestershire sauce, and water in a small sauce-pan; bring to a boil. Add peanuts; let stand for 30 minutes. Drain off liquid; spread nuts in a shallow baking pan and bake at 250° for 1 hour. Toss nuts with butter and drain on paper towels. Sprinkle with garlic salt. Yield: 4 servings.

CURRIED PEANUTS

1 pound salted peanuts
3 or 4 tablespoons curry
   powder

Put peanuts in a shallow pan. Bake at 300° for 15 to 20 minutes, stirring occasionally to prevent burning. Remove and, while still hot, stir in curry powder. Cool and place in an airtight container. Yield: 1 pound.

PARCHED PEANUTS

Put dried peanuts in hulls in a shallow pan. Bake at 350° for 30 minutes, stirring occasionally. To test to see if they are parched, remove one from oven. Let cool; if crunchy, peanuts are ready. Different size nuts vary a little in time of cooking.

COCKTAIL PECANS

2 tablespoons butter or
   margarine
½ teaspoon seasoned salt
1 or 2 dashes of hot pepper
   sauce

1 pound pecan halves
3 tablespoons Worcestershire
   sauce

Put butter, seasoned salt, and hot pepper sauce in a 12- x 8- x 2-inch baking dish. Place in a 300° oven until butter melts. Add pecans, stirring until all are butter coated. Bake for about 20 minutes, stirring occasionally. Sprinkle with Worcestershire sauce; stir again and continue baking another 15 minutes or until crisp. Will freeze. Yield: about 1 pound.

JALAPEÑO COCKTAIL PIE

2 or 3 jalapeño peppers,
  seeded and chopped
4 cups shredded sharp
  Cheddar cheese

6 eggs, beaten

Sprinkle peppers in a well-greased 9-inch square pan; cover with cheese. Pour eggs over cheese. Bake at 350° for 30 minutes or until firm. Cool and cut into 1-inch squares. Yield: about 6½ dozen.

Jalapeño Cocktail Pie (above)

PARTY POPCORN

2 cups miniature marshmallows
⅓ to ½ cup melted butter or margarine
3 quarts unsalted popped corn
1 (3-ounce) package fruit-flavored gelatin

Combine marshmallows and butter in the top of a double boiler; cook over simmering water until marshmallows have melted. Pour over popped corn and stir to mix well. Sprinkle gelatin over popcorn and stir to coat each kernel. Yield: 3½ quarts.

POPCORN CRUMBLE

2 quarts unsalted popped corn
1⅓ cups pecan halves
⅔ cup sliced almonds
1⅓ cups sugar
1 cup butter or margarine
½ cup white corn syrup
2 teaspoons vanilla extract

Mix popcorn and nuts in a large bowl and set aside. Combine sugar, butter, and corn syrup in a heavy saucepan. Bring to a boil; stir constantly and cook to 300°, using a candy thermometer.

Add vanilla and very quickly pour over popcorn and nut mixture. Stir to coat well and spread on a greased cookie sheet to harden.

When mixture has cooled, break into serving-size pieces. Yield: about 1 pound.

ROAST PORK STRIPS

½ cup soy sauce
¼ cup bourbon
½ teaspoon ground ginger
3 tablespoons honey
1 clove garlic, crushed
1 (3-pound) pork tenderloin
Lettuce or parsley
Grapefruit, apple, or pineapple, cut into pieces (optional)

Combine soy sauce, bourbon, ginger, honey, and garlic. Place pork in a shallow glass dish and pour marinade over it. Cover and refrigerate overnight, turning the meat occasionally.

Place meat in a shallow baking dish and bake at 300° for about 1½ hours, spooning marinade over meat from time to time.

To serve as an appetizer, allow meat to cool, then cut into thin slices (about ⅛ inch thick). Cut slices into strips and spear each with a wooden pick. Arrange on a bed of lettuce or parsley—or insert picks into a grapefruit or apple or pineapple.

This pork is best served at room temperature. The flavor is subtle and the pork requires no dipping sauce to enhance it. Yield: 12 servings.

PRETZEL POPS

1 (3-ounce) package cream
   cheese, softened
2 ounces blue cheese,
   crumbled
1 (2¼-ounce) can deviled
   ham

¼ cup chopped pecans
⅛ teaspoon onion powder
1 cup chopped parsley
Thin pretzel sticks

Combine first 5 ingredients. Chill. Make bite-size balls, using about 1 teaspoonful of mixture for each. Roll in parsley. Use pretzel sticks as toothpicks. Chill until ready to serve. Yield: 2 dozen.

BEEF SAUSAGE STACKS

2 (3-ounce) packages cream
   cheese, softened
2 teaspoons prepared
   horseradish, drained
1 teaspoon chopped parsley

2 tablespoons grated onion
1 pound smoked beef sausage,
   thinly sliced

Combine cream cheese, horseradish, parsley, and onion; mix well. Spread 7 slices of beef sausage with cream cheese mixture, stacking them to form a cylinder. Top with a slice of sausage. Repeat for each cylinder. Wrap in waxed paper and chill for 3 hours or more. When ready to serve, cut each stack into 6 or 8 wedges. Yield: 42 to 56 appetizers.

MARINATED SHRIMP

1¼ cups olive oil
¾ cup vinegar
2½ tablespoons capers
2½ teaspoons celery seeds
1½ teaspoons salt
7 or 8 bay leaves

Dash of hot sauce
1 medium onion, thinly sliced
5 pounds medium shrimp,
   cooked, peeled, and
   deveined

Combine all ingredients except shrimp; stir until well blended. Pour marinade over shrimp. Cover and chill at least 8 hours. Remove bay leaves before serving. Yield: 20 to 25 appetizer servings.

Photograph for this recipe on page 154

PICKLED SHRIMP

3 to 4 pounds large raw
   shrimp in the shell
½ cup chopped celery tops
¼ cup mixed pickling spices

3½ teaspoons salt
2 cups sliced onion
7 or 8 bay leaves
Marinade

Put shrimp in a large saucepan; cover with boiling water. Add celery tops, pickling spices, and salt. Cover and simmer for 5 minutes. Drain. Cool by immersing in cold water; peel and devein.

In a shallow bowl, alternate shrimp with 2 cups sliced onion and 7 or 8 bay leaves. Serve shrimp with Marinade. Yield: 15 servings.

Marinade:

1¼ cups salad oil	1½ teaspoons celery seed
¾ cup vinegar	1½ teaspoons salt
1½ tablespoons capers, including juice	Dash of hot pepper sauce

Combine marinade ingredients; mix well and pour over shrimp. Cover; chill at least 24 hours. Serve shrimp in bowl with marinade and provide wooden picks and small plates. Pickled shrimp will keep at least a week in the refrigerator. Yield: about 2 cups.

SCAMPI

2 pounds peeled and deveined shrimp	¾ teaspoon salt
⅓ cup olive oil	½ teaspoon pepper
½ cup vermouth	3 tablespoons chopped parsley
2 cloves garlic, crushed	3 tablespoons lemon juice

Sauté shrimp in hot oil. Add vermouth, garlic, salt, and pepper; simmer until liquid is almost absorbed. Sprinkle with parsley and lemon juice; stir gently to mix. Yield: about 10 to 12 appetizer servings.

Scampi (above)

SEA ISLAND SHRIMP

2 to 3 pounds raw shrimp
2 unpeeled lemons, sliced
  paper-thin
1 large onion, sliced
  paper-thin
1⅓ cups olive oil

⅔ cup tarragon vinegar
Juice of 2 lemons
2 teaspoons salt
Pepper

Boil and devein shrimp; slice if desired. Place in a bowl with lemon and onion slices. Place all other ingredients in a jar with a tight-fitting cover and shake vigorously; pour over shrimp. Cover and refrigerate overnight. Serve shrimp in marinade with wooden picks for spearing. Yield: 8 to 10 servings.

SHRIMP ARNAUD

¼ cup vinegar
¼ cup salad oil
¼ cup chili sauce
¼ teaspoon garlic salt

1 teaspoon prepared mustard
1 pound shrimp, cooked and
  peeled

Combine vinegar, salad oil, chili sauce, garlic salt, and mustard. Add shrimp and toss to coat with sauce. Marinate overnight. Insert a wooden pick in each shrimp before serving. Yield: 6 servings.

SHRIMP COCKTAIL

2 pounds boiled shrimp
½ cup olive oil
¼ cup paprika
1 tablespoon prepared
  horseradish
1 tablespoon prepared mustard

¼ cup tarragon vinegar
1 teaspoon celery seed
½ teaspoon salt
⅛ teaspoon pepper
½ teaspoon onion salt
Dash of hot pepper sauce

Chill shrimp and place in cocktail cups around cracked ice. Combine other ingredients and serve in a small container in middle of shrimp. Yield: 6 servings.

ZESTY SHRIMP COCKTAIL

1 cup chili sauce
1 cup catsup
2 tablespoons prepared
  horseradish
2 tablespoons vinegar
1 tablespoon Worcestershire
  sauce

2 teaspoons lemon juice
Dash of hot sauce
Fresh cooked shrimp
Lemon wedges (optional)

Combine all ingredients except shrimp and lemon wedges, mixing well. Chill sauce at least half an hour before serving. Serve with shrimp, and garnish with lemon wedges, if desired. Yield: about 2 cups.

Zesty Shrimp Cocktail (page 78)

MARINATED SHRIMP PORT GIBSON

5 pounds raw shrimp in shell, cooked and cleaned	1 clove garlic, minced
1 cup salad oil	5 tablespoons minced fresh parsley
½ cup vinegar	¾ cup horseradish mustard
1¼ cups minced celery	1½ teaspoons salt
2½ tablespoons minced green pepper	¼ teaspoon pepper
¼ cup grated onion	¼ cup paprika

Place shrimp in a deep bowl. Mix other ingredients thoroughly and pour over shrimp. Cover and marinate in refrigerator for 24 hours before serving, stirring occasionally. This shrimp may be used as an appetizer, first course, or main dish salad. Yield: 10 to 12 servings.

STUFFED CHERRY TOMATOES

1 cup pot-style cottage or
  cream cheese
1 tablespoon chopped chives
2 teaspoons Worcestershire
  sauce

Salt and pepper to taste
18 cherry tomatoes
Parsley flakes

Combine cottage cheese, chives, Worcestershire sauce, salt, and pepper; blend well. Scoop out inside pulp of cherry tomatoes. Fill shell with cheese mixture. Granish with parsley flakes. Yield: 1½ dozen.

Note: The cherry tomato shell makes a pretty "holder" for many fillings. Ideas for fillings include egg salad, crab or shrimp salad, and guacamole.

Photograph for this recipe on cover

TOTE'MS

Deviled Ham Tote'ms:

2 (4½-ounce) cans deviled
  ham
1 (3-ounce) package cream
  cheese, softened
1 tablespoon minced onion
¼ cup finely chopped celery
4 teaspoons finely chopped
  pimiento

3 tablespoons drained pickle
  relish
1 teaspoon prepared mustard
2 (10-inch) submarine rolls (2
  inches wide)

Liverwurst Spread Tote'ms:

2 (4¾-ounce) cans liverwurst
  spread
1 (3-ounce) package cream
  cheese, softened
1 tablespoon prepared mustard

⅓ cup finely chopped dill
  pickle
2 (10-inch) submarine rolls (2
  inches wide)

Chicken Spread Tote'ms:

2 (4¾-ounce) cans chicken
  spread
1 (3-ounce) package cream
  cheese, softened
2 hard-cooked eggs, finely
  chopped
¼ cup finely chopped celery
2 tablespoons finely chopped
  parsley

4 teaspoons finely chopped
  pimiento
½ teaspoon Worcestershire
  sauce
¼ to ½ teaspoon salt
2 (10-inch) submarine rolls (2
  inches wide)

For each variation, combine all ingredients except rolls. Cut rolls in half vertically. Using a sharp knife and a fork, hollow out rolls almost to tip of each half, leaving a ¼-inch shell. (Save scooped-out bread for stuffings, meatloaf, etc.) Fill with meat spread mixture, pressing filling firmly to eliminate air spaces. Wrap stuffed bread halves, cut ends together, and chill well, preferably overnight. Cut into ¼-inch slices; keep chilled until served. Yield: about 4 dozen.

SPICED WALNUTS

1 cup sugar	
1 teaspoon salt	¼ teaspoon ground cloves
2 teaspoons ground cinnamon	½ cup water
½ teaspoon ground nutmeg	2½ cups walnut halves

Combine sugar, salt, and spices in a heavy saucepan; stir in ½ cup water. Cook, stirring constantly, over medium heat until sugar dissolves; cook to soft ball stage (230°). Remove from heat, and stir in walnuts. Stir until mixture becomes creamy.

Spread on waxed paper, and separate nuts with a fork. Cool. Yield: 2½ cups.

TOASTED WALNUTS

Drop shelled walnuts into rapidly boiling water; boil for 3 minutes. Drain well. Spread kernels evenly in a shallow pan and bake at 350°, stirring often, for 12 to 15 minutes or until kernels are a golden brown. If you like seasoned walnuts, lightly brush the hot kernels with butter and sprinkle with salt, garlic salt, onion salt, or seasoned salt. Cool. Cover tightly and store in the refrigerator.

WALNUT FIREBALLS

2 (3-ounce) packages cream cheese with chives, softened	½ cup finely chopped walnuts
	1 cup minced spiced luncheon meat
1½ teaspoons prepared horseradish	

Combine cream cheese and horseradish, mixing well; stir in walnuts. Shape mixture into 1-inch balls; roll each in minced luncheon meat. Chill. Serve on toothpicks. Yield: 3 dozen.

Clockwise: Avocado Dip (page 84); Sausage-Bacon Roll-ups (page 46); Chicken Liver Pâté (page 135); Buttercup Cheese Straws (page 64)

dips & spreads

As summer approaches and casual entertaining increases, you are often called upon to serve appetizers on short notice. Chances are you'll whip up some dips and spreads because they are quick and easy to prepare.

A big advantage in serving dips and spreads is that they can be made ahead of time. In fact, most improve if allowed to stand before serving as it gives the flavors a chance to blend.

Imaginative accompaniments can make the most everyday dips and spreads taste special. Crisp vegetables, such as carrots, cauliflower, cucumber, celery, and squash, are favorites of many guests.

If you prefer chips, crackers, or toast rounds as accompaniments, make sure they are fresh and crisp. Freshness can be restored to crackers and chips by heating at 250° about 20 minutes. When selecting crackers, choose those that are rather neutral tasting so they don't compete with the flavor of the dip or spread.

ARTICHOKE DIP

1 (16-ounce) can artichoke
   hearts, drained
About ⅓ cup mayonnaise
1 tablespoon chopped onion
Salt, black pepper, and
   cayenne pepper to taste

3 or 4 slices bacon, cooked
   crisp and finely crumbled
Juice of ½ lemon
Corn chips

Chop artichoke hearts to a pulp. Add other ingredients (except corn chips) and stir well; check seasonings and correct if necessary. Chill. Serve with corn chips for dipping. Yield: about 1½ cups.

ARTICHOKE-BLUE CHEESE DIP

1 (15-ounce) can artichoke
   hearts, drained
¼ cup commercial sour cream
1 teaspoon crumbled blue
   cheese
½ teaspoon onion salt

1¼ teaspoons lemon juice
¼ teaspoon paprika
1½ teaspoons sugar
Crackers

Blend artichoke hearts, sour cream, and blue cheese in blender. Add remaining ingredients except crackers. Refrigerate until ready to serve with crackers. Yield: about 1⅓ cups.

AVOCADO DIP

1 avocado, mashed
1 (8-ounce) package cream
   cheese, softened
2 tablespoons lemon juice
Dash of Worcestershire sauce

⅓ cup minced green onion
¾ teaspoon salt
2 green chiles, mashed
Corn chips

Blend avocado into cheese until smooth. Add other ingredients except corn chips and blend well. Cover and chill. Serve with corn chips. Yield: about 2 cups.

Note: This dip may be prepared ahead of time, even the day before serving. Spread a thin layer of mayonnaise over surface to prevent darkening; stir it in just before serving.

Photograph for this recipe on page 82

CREAMY AVOCADO DIP

2 cups mashed avocado
1 tablespoon minced onion
1 clove garlic, minced
¼ teaspoon chili powder
¼ teaspoon salt

Dash of pepper
⅓ cup mayonnaise
6 slices bacon, cooked and
   crumbled

Combine avocado, onion, garlic, chili powder, salt, and pepper; blend well. Place in a small bowl; cover with mayonnaise, spreading over top and sides to keep avocado from turning dark. Refrigerate for several hours to blend flavors. When ready to serve, mix well and sprinkle top with crumbled bacon. Yield: 1⅓ cups.

DILLY AVOCADO DIP

2 avocados
1 (8-ounce) carton cottage
  cheese
½ teaspoon grated onion
2 tablespoons chopped dill
  pickle

2 tablespoons chopped parsley
1 tablespoon lemon juice
¾ teaspoon salt
⅛ teaspoon dillweed

Cut avocados lengthwise into halves; remove seeds and skin. Cut into chunks; mash or sieve avocado. Stir in remaining ingredients. If dip is not to be served immediately, cover at once. Chill. Yield: about 2½ cups.

AVOCADO AND BACON DIP

1 ripe avocado, peeled and
  pitted
2 teaspoons lemon juice
¼ cup commercial sour cream
1 teaspoon instant minced
  onion

¼ teaspoon garlic salt
¼ teaspoon paprika
¼ cup crumbled bacon
Crackers

Mash avocado. Add remaining ingredients except crackers. Cover tightly; refrigerate until ready to serve with crackers. Yield: about 1¼ cups.

ZESTY BACON DIP

4 to 6 slices bacon
1 (8-ounce) carton commercial
  sour cream
1 tablespoon prepared
  horseradish

1 teaspoon Worcestershire
  sauce
Corn chips, potato chips, or
  crackers

Cook bacon until crisp; drain and crumble. Combine all ingredients except chips. Serve as a dip with corn chips, potato chips, or crackers. Yield: 1 cup.

BAKED BEEF DIP

1 cup chopped pecans
2 teaspoons melted butter or margarine
2 (8-ounce) packages cream cheese, softened
¼ cup milk

2 (2½-ounce) packages dried beef, minced
½ teaspoon garlic salt
1 (8-ounce) carton commercial sour cream
4 teaspoons minced onion

Sauté pecans in butter until lightly browned; drain and set aside. Combine remaining ingredients, mixing well. Spoon into a greased 1½-quart baking dish; top with pecans.

Bake at 350° for 20 minutes or until thoroughly heated. Serve hot with assorted crackers, chips, or breadsticks. Yield: about 4 cups.

CHEESE DIP

1 envelope unflavored gelatin
1 cup buttermilk, divided
2 cups cottage cheese
¼ pound Roquefort cheese, crumbled

1 small onion, finely chopped
1 small clove garlic, finely chopped
¼ teaspoon salt

Soften gelatin in ¼ cup buttermilk; place over hot water and stir until gelatin is dissolved. Combine gelatin mixture with remaining ingredients in a small bowl. Beat with an electric mixer or a rotary beater until smooth and creamy. Serve with assorted vegetable dippers. If mixture stiffens while standing, whip again until smooth. Yield: about 3½ cups.

HOT CHEESE DIP

1 pound process cheese spread, cubed

¼ cup plus 2 tablespoons picante sauce

Melt cubed cheese in top of a double boiler; stir in picante sauce. Serve hot with corn chips or tortilla chips. Yield: 2 cups.

ANCHOVY-CHEESE DIP

2 (3-ounce) packages cream
    cheese, softened
2 tablespoons butter or
    margarine, softened
⅓ cup mayonnaise
1 tablespoon anchovy paste
1 teaspoon paprika

1 teaspoon Worcestershire
    sauce
1 tablespoon grated onion
½ teaspoon caraway seed
Salt, if required
1 or 2 dashes of cayenne
    pepper

Blend cream cheese and softened butter together. Blend in mayonnaise
gradually, then all other ingredients until of dipping consistency. (If you
prefer a spread, reduce amount of mayonnaise.) Yield: about 1½ cups.

   Note: This dip may be made a day ahead of time, but refrigeration makes
the mixture stiff and buttery in consistency. It may be served that way, but
it is also attractive to beat it with an electric mixer until fluffy. Serve with
plain melba toast.

SUPER BEAN-CHEESE DIP

1 (11-ounce) can black bean
    soup, undiluted
1 teaspoon prepared mustard
½ teaspoon thyme
1 clove garlic

1 (8-ounce) package cream
    cheese, softened
Corn chips, celery, carrots,
    and cauliflower

Combine soup, mustard, thyme, and garlic in a blender. Add chunks of
cream cheese, blending until smooth. Chill for several hours. Serve with
corn chips, celery and carrot sticks, and cauliflower buds. Yield: about 2
cups.

▪ *Candles should be used only after sundown or on a dark, gloomy day. If candles
are on the table, always light them.*

▪ *To make shredding of very soft cheese easier, put in the freezer for 15 minutes.*

▪ *Refrigerator space will be at a premium. Make sure you have enough shelf space
for cold foods as well as for storage of foods prepared ahead. Turn the refrigerator
to its coldest setting without freezing to compensate for the extra food.*

BEER KEG DIP

½ (8-ounce) package cream
   cheese, softened
1 (4-ounce) package blue
   cheese, crumbled
2 cups shredded sharp
   Cheddar cheese
2 tablespoons butter or
   margarine, softened

1 teaspoon grated onion
¼ teaspoon salt
¾ cup beer
Dash of Worcestershire sauce

Combine cheeses and butter; beat by hand or with electric mixer until smooth. Blend in onion and salt; slowly beat in beer. Add Worcestershire sauce; blend well. Pack into a jar, cover tightly, and refrigerate for at least 12 hours. Remove from refrigerator 30 minutes before serving. Yield: about 2½ cups.

CAVIAR-CHEESE DIP

1 (8-ounce) package cream
   cheese, softened
3 tablespoons commercial
   sour cream
2 tablespoons minced chives
   or onions

2 tablespoons lemon juice
1 tablespoon Worcestershire
   sauce
3 tablespoons red caviar
Paprika

Blend cheese and sour cream. Add chives, lemon juice, and Worcestershire sauce; mix well. Gently stir in caviar; sprinkle top with paprika before serving. Yield: about 1 cup.

PEANUT BUTTER-CHEESE DIP

½ cup chopped onion
1 cup chopped green pepper
1 clove garlic, chopped
2 tablespoons peanut oil
2 tomatoes, peeled and
   chopped
¾ cup tomato juice
¼ teaspoon thyme
¼ teaspoon oregano

½ bay leaf
2 cups shredded Cheddar
   cheese
¾ cup peanut butter (smooth
   or crunchy)
½ teaspoon salt
⅛ teaspoon pepper
Corn chips or potato chips

Cook onion, green pepper, and garlic in peanut oil until tender, but not browned. Add tomatoes, tomato juice, thyme, oregano, and bay leaf; cover and cook over low heat for 10 minutes. Stir once or twice. Put in top of double boiler and add cheese, peanut butter, salt, and pepper. Cook and stir over boiling water until cheese is melted and mixture is blended. Serve in a chafing dish with corn or potato chips. Yield: 4 cups.

COPENHAGEN DUNKER'S DELIGHT

½ cup commercial sour cream
¼ cup mayonnaise
2 tablespoons chopped dill
  pickle

¼ teaspoon onion juice
¼ teaspoon dry mustard

Combine sour cream and mayonnaise; add dill pickle, onion juice, and mustard. Mix well. Chill. Yield: ¾ cup.

COTTAGE CHEESE DUNK FOR VEGETABLES

2 (8-ounce) cartons cottage
  cheese
1 cup shredded process
  American cheese
2 tablespoons prepared
  horseradish
2 tablespoons minced onion

2 tablespoons chopped green
  pepper
3 tablespoons mayonnaise
¼ teaspoon salt
½ teaspoon pepper

Combine all ingredients; chill and serve with raw vegetables. Yield: about 4 cups.

CURRIED COTTAGE CHEESE DIP

1 cup creamed cottage cheese
¼ cup sweet pickle relish,
  drained

¼ teaspoon curry powder
1 teaspoon grated onion
Paprika

Put cottage cheese through a sieve or food mill; combine with other ingredients except paprika. Mix well. Cover and refrigerate for about 1 hour. Spoon into a serving dish and sprinkle with paprika. Yield: about 1 cup.

CRACKER BARREL CHEESE DIP

2 cups shredded sharp
  process American cheese
½ cup finely diced celery
¼ cup chili sauce
¼ cup finely diced onion

¼ cup finely diced green
  pepper
¼ cup minced green olives
Half-and-half

Blend first 6 ingredients. Mix thoroughly with enough half-and-half to make a smooth and light dip. Chill. Yield: about 3 cups.

SPICY CREAM CHEESE DIP

1 (8-ounce) package cream
  cheese, softened
¼ cup picante sauce

Juice of ½ lemon
Salt and pepper to taste

Combine all ingredients, blending well. Serve with corn chips, tortilla chips, potato chips, or crackers. Yield: about 1 cup.

DEVILED CHEESE BITES

2 (3-ounce) packages cream
  cheese, softened
1 (4-ounce) package blue
  cheese, crumbled
2 (2¼-ounce) cans deviled
  ham
½ cup chopped pecans

Onion juice to taste
½ to 1 cup finely chopped
  parsley
½ cup commercial sour cream
Garlic salt to taste
Thin pretzel sticks

Combine cream cheese and blue cheese; blend until smooth. Stir in deviled ham, pecans, and onion juice; chill. Shape into balls the size of walnuts, and roll them in parsley; chill until serving time.

  Combine sour cream and garlic salt; chill. Serve as a dip, and use pretzel sticks to spear cheese balls. Yield: about 40 appetizers.

SWISS DIP

2 cups shredded Swiss cheese
1 (4½-ounce) can deviled
  ham

¼ cup catsup
¼ cup bourbon
Assorted chips or breadsticks

Melt cheese over hot water; add deviled ham, catsup, and bourbon. Serve hot with chips or breadsticks. Yield: 2 cups.

CHILI-CHEESE DIP

1 medium onion, finely
  chopped
3 slices bacon, chopped
1 pound process American
  cheese, cubed

1 (15-ounce) can chili without
  beans
1 (10-ounce) can tomatoes
  with hot peppers, chopped

Sauté onion and bacon until onion is tender. Stir in remaining ingredients; heat until bubbly, stirring well. Serve warm with corn chips. Yield: about 3½ cups.

JALAPEÑO CHEESE DIP

2 tablespoons all-purpose flour
¾ cup half-and-half
3 tablespoons butter or
  margarine
2 pounds process cheese, cut
  into pieces
1 pint cottage cheese

1 medium onion, finely
  chopped
1 medium green pepper, finely
  chopped
1 clove garlic, minced
4 jalapeño peppers

Combine flour and half-and-half in double boiler. Add butter and cheeses; melt. Add remaining ingredients and simmer 10 to 15 minutes or until thick, stirring occasionally. If desired, serve warm as a dip or as a spread for crackers and sandwiches. Yield: about 3 cups.

HOT CHILI DIP

1 (15-ounce) can chili without
  beans
1 cup shredded Cheddar
  cheese

Hot sauce to taste
½ teaspoon cayenne pepper

Combine all ingredients; heat until cheese melts. Serve hot with tortilla chips or corn chips. Yield: about 2 cups.

Hot Chili Dip (above)

Mexi-Chile Dip (below)

MEXI-CHILE DIP

1 (3-ounce) can pitted black olives, chopped
1 (4-ounce) can green chiles, chopped
1 medium onion, chopped

1 large tomato, chopped
1½ tablespoons vinegar
3 tablespoons olive oil
1 teaspoon garlic salt

Combine first 4 ingredients in a small bowl. Combine remaining ingredients, and add to vegetable mixture. Chill at least 2 hours before serving. Serve with corn chips. Yield: 2½ cups.

CHILE CON QUESO

2 pounds process cheese, shredded
2 large onions, minced
1 (16-ounce) can whole tomatoes, drained and chopped
2 small cloves garlic, minced

2 (4-ounce) cans green chile peppers, drained and mashed
2 tablespoons Worcestershire sauce
Corn chips

Melt cheese in the top of a double boiler over hot water. Blend in other ingredients except corn chips and cook for 30 minutes, stirring occasionally. Serve in a chafing dish with corn chips for dipping. Any leftover dip may be frozen successfully. To use again, allow to thaw at room temperature; then reheat in the top of a double boiler. Yield: about 6 cups.

CHILE CON QUESO DIP

1 (10½-ounce) can tomatoes
with hot peppers
4 cups shredded process
American cheese

Crackers, corn chips, or potato
chips

Combine tomatoes and cheese in top of a double boiler. Cook over simmering water until cheese has melted. Stir mixture occasionally. Serve hot or cold with crackers, corn chips, or potato chips. Yield: about 2 cups.

CLAMDIGGER DIP

1 (7½-ounce) can minced
clams
1 (8-ounce) package cream
cheese, softened
1 tablespoon lemon juice
1 teaspoon Worcestershire
sauce

1 tablespoon grated onion
1 teaspoon chopped parsley
¼ teaspoon salt
⅛ teaspoon hot pepper sauce
Assorted chips, crackers, or
raw vegetables

Drain clams and reserve liquor. Combine cream cheese and lemon juice. Add seasonings and clams. Mix thoroughly. Chill for at least 1 hour to blend flavors. If it is necessary to thin the dip, add clam liquor gradually. Serve with chips, crackers, or vegetables. Yield: 1⅓ cups.

CLAM-CREAM CHEESE DIP

6 (3-ounce) packages cream
cheese
3 (7-ounce) cans clams,
drained and liquor reserved

1 large onion, grated
Lemon juice
Crackers or potato chips

Soften cream cheese thoroughly. Add clams, onion, and lemon juice (start with juice of 1 lemon, adding more to taste) or use reserved clam liquor to moisten the mixture. Turn into a chafing dish and serve hot, with crackers or sturdy potato chips for dipping. This amount will serve a crowd, the size depending on the number of other appetizers offered. Leftover mixture will freeze satisfactorily. Yield: about 5 cups.

• *Freeze extra parsley in plastic bags; just snip off sprigs of frozen parsley as needed.*

• *Crush leftover potato chips or pretzels, and use as toppings for other dishes.*

CLAM AND CHEESE DIP

1 (7-ounce) can minced clams
2 (3-ounce) packages cream
   cheese, softened
2 teaspoons grated onion
2 teaspoons lemon juice

1 teaspoon Worcestershire
   sauce
1 teaspoon chopped parsley
¼ teaspoon salt
3 drops of hot pepper sauce

Drain clams and save liquor. Combine all ingredients except liquor; blend into a paste. Gradually add about ¼ cup clam liquor and beat until consistency of whipped cream. Chill. Serve in a bowl. Yield: about 2 cups.

CURRIED MERMAID DIP

2 (3-ounce) packages cream
   cheese, softened
1 (8-ounce) can minced
   clams, drained
1 (2-ounce) jar pimientos,
   drained and chopped
¼ cup finely chopped nuts

¼ cup finely chopped celery
¼ cup commercial sour cream
½ teaspoon curry powder
½ teaspoon seasoned salt
Chopped parsley
Assorted crackers

Blend first 8 ingredients. Chill. Sprinkle with parsley and serve with crackers. Yield: 1¾ cups.

CHRISTMAS CRAB DIP

1 (8-ounce) package cream
   cheese, softened
1 (6½-ounce) can crab claw
   meat, drained

1 teaspoon mayonnaise
Paprika
Parsley sprigs

Blend cream cheese, crabmeat, and mayonnaise. Sprinkle with paprika and chill before serving. Garnish with parsley sprigs. Yield: 1½ cups.

DEVILED CRAB DIP

1 (7¾-ounce) can crabmeat,
   drained and flaked
1 hard-cooked egg, chopped
½ cup mayonnaise
1 tablespoon lemon juice

½ teaspoon dry mustard
½ teaspoon onion salt
⅛ teaspoon pepper
Assorted crackers

Combine all ingredients except crackers; mix well. Cover and chill. Serve with assorted snack crackers. Yield: 2 cups.

GREEN GODDESS CRAB DIP

4 anchovy fillets, chopped
2 tablespoons finely chopped
   onion
2 tablespoons chopped chives
¼ cup finely chopped parsley
¼ teaspoon salt

½ teaspoon dry mustard
⅛ teaspoon pepper
¼ cup tarragon vinegar
1 cup mayonnaise
Bite-size pieces of crab

Combine all ingredients except crab in a bowl, mixing well. Cover and refrigerate for several hours or overnight to blend flavors. Serve as dip for bite-size pieces of crab on wooden picks. Yield: about ½ cup.

RED DIP FOR CRAB ON ICE

1 cup catsup
½ cup chili sauce
¼ teaspoon hot pepper sauce
1½ teaspoons Worcestershire
   sauce
1 tablespoon prepared
   horseradish

1½ teaspoons prepared
   mustard
2 tablespoons lemon juice
Chopped parsley

Combine all ingredients except parsley. Chill for at least 1 hour to blend flavors. Serve, garnished with parsley, as a dip for crab. Yield: about 1½ cups.

HOT CRABMEAT DIP

1 (8-ounce) package cream
   cheese
3 tablespoons mayonnaise
1 teaspoon Dijon mustard
¼ teaspoon salt

2 tablespoons dry white wine
1 (7¾-ounce) can crabmeat,
   drained and flaked
Melba rounds or toast triangles

Combine cream cheese, mayonnaise, mustard, and salt in top of a double boiler over simmering water. Stir until smooth and well blended. Add wine gradually, then crabmeat; check seasonings. Transfer to a chafing dish and serve hot with melba rounds or toast triangles for dipping. Yield: about 2 cups.

CURRIED CRABMEAT DIP

1 (7-ounce) can crabmeat,
    drained
½ (8-ounce) package cream
    cheese, softened
5 tablespoons commercial
    sour cream

¼ teaspoon salt
Pepper to taste
¼ teaspoon curry powder
1 tablespoon minced chives
1 tablespoon capers, drained
Potato chips or melba rounds

Finely shred crabmeat. Combine cheese with other ingredients except crabmeat, capers, and potato chips and beat until light. Fold in crabmeat and capers; chill and serve with potato chips or melba rounds for dipping. Yield: about 2 cups.

CUCUMBER DIP

2 large unpeeled cucumbers
½ cup vinegar
2 teaspoons salt
½ teaspoon garlic salt

2 (8-ounce) packages cream
    cheese, softened
¾ cup mayonnaise

Wash and grate unpeeled cucumbers, using grater with ½-inch holes. Add vinegar and salt; stir, cover, and allow to stand overnight in refrigerator. Next day, press out liquid. Blend garlic salt, cheese, and mayonnaise; combine with cucumbers. Yield: about 4 cups.

FRUIT STICKS WITH CURRY DIP GREGNON

Cut into finger-size pieces any firm fruit, such as melon, pineapple, apples, or pears. Chill thoroughly and place on a platter around Curry Dip Gregnon. Strawberries may be used with wooden picks inserted.

Curry Dip Gregnon:

1 cup mayonnaise
2 to 4 tablespoons curry
    powder

3 tablespoons lemon juice
1 tablespoon chutney
Dash of hot pepper sauce

Mix all ingredients thoroughly in a blender. Chill well. Yield: 1½ cups.

ZESTY FRESH GARDEN DIP

1 (3-ounce) package cream
    cheese, softened
¼ cup mayonnaise
3 tablespoons commercial
    sour cream
2 tablespoons grated
    cucumber

2 tablespoons grated radishes
¼ teaspoon grated onion
¼ teaspoon dry mustard
Salt and pepper to taste
Assorted crackers

Combine cream cheese, mayonnaise, sour cream, cucumber, radishes, onion, mustard, salt, and pepper. Blend thoroughly. Cover and chill. Serve with assorted crackers. Yield: about 1 cup.

DELUXE DIP

¼ cup commercial French
  dressing
¾ cup commercial sour cream

¼ teaspoon pepper (optional)
1 tablespoon chopped chives

Blend French dressing, sour cream, pepper (if desired), and chives. Serve chilled. Yield: 1 cup.

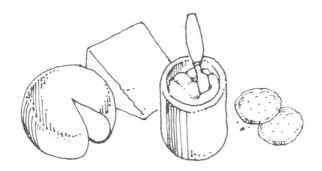

DILL DIP

1 (3-ounce) package cream
  cheese, softened
1 tablespoon finely chopped
  stuffed green olives
1 teaspoon grated onion

¼ teaspoon dillweed
Dash of salt
1 to 2 tablespoons
  half-and-half
Raw zucchini, cut into sticks

Combine cream cheese, olives, onion, dillweed, and salt; stir in half-and-half to make mixture of dipping consistency. Chill. Serve with zucchini sticks as an appetizer. Yield: about ⅔ cup.

DILL DIP FOR RAW VEGETABLES

1 cup mayonnaise
2 (8-ounce) cartons
  commercial sour cream
2 tablespoons dillweed

1 tablespoon minced parsley
Salt, if needed
Raw vegetables
Lemon juice

Gently combine mayonnaise and other ingredients except raw vegetables and lemon juice. Serve in a bowl surrounded by crisp raw vegetables: cauliflower flowerets, celery sticks, carrot sticks, cherry tomatoes, and zucchini slices. Yield: about 3 cups.

Photograph for this recipe on page 105

SMOKED EGG DIP

12 hard-cooked eggs, finely
   chopped
2 tablespoons butter or
   margarine, softened
1½ teaspoons liquid smoke
1 tablespoon lemon juice or
   vinegar
2 teaspoons prepared mustard

2 teaspoons Worcestershire
   sauce
8 drops hot sauce
1¼ teaspoons salt
½ teaspoon pepper
1 cup mayonnaise or salad
   dressing
3 thinly sliced radishes

Combine all ingredients except radishes; beat at medium speed of electric mixer until smooth. Chill at least 1 hour; beat until fluffy.

Garnish with radish slices; serve with vegetables, crackers, or chips. Yield: about 4 cups.

Photograph for this recipe on page 140

CAPONATA

3 large eggplants, peeled and
   cubed
Salt
8 stalks celery, chopped
3 medium onions, chopped
3 tablespoons olive oil

4 (8-ounce) cans tomato
   sauce
2 (2-ounce) jars capers,
   drained
1 (5-ounce) jar stuffed olives,
   drained and sliced

Sprinkle eggplant with salt; set aside. Sauté celery and onion in oil until tender; add tomato sauce, and simmer 15 minutes.

Squeeze eggplant, and rinse well; add to tomato mixture. Cook over medium heat, stirring occasionally, about 1½ to 2 hours or until eggplant is very soft. Stir in capers and olives; simmer 15 minutes. Serve hot or cold with crackers. Yield: about 8 cups.

SMOKY FISH DIP

¾ pound smoked fish
1 (8-ounce) package cream
   cheese, softened
2 tablespoons half-and-half

2 tablespoons lemon juice
½ teaspoon liquid smoke
¼ teaspoon garlic salt
Assorted crackers or chips

Remove skin and bones from fish. Chop fish very fine. Combine all ingredients except crackers; mix thoroughly. Chill. Serve with assorted crackers or chips. Yield: 2 cups.

▪ *Using kitchen shears for cutting many foods saves time and gives a neat-looking cut. When cutting sticky foods like marshmallows or dates, dip the shears in hot water.*

GREAT LAKES DIP

½ pound smoked whitefish or
   other smoked fish
1 (8-ounce) carton commercial
   sour cream
2 tablespoons lemon juice
1 teaspoon instant minced
   onion
2 teaspoons chopped chives

½ teaspoon salt
¼ teaspoon rosemary
6 peppercorns, crushed
Dash of ground cloves
Chopped parsley
Assorted chips, crackers, or
   raw vegetables

Remove skin and bones from fish. Flake fish. Combine all ingredients except parsley and crackers. Chill for at least 1 hour to blend flavors. Sprinkle dip with parsley. Serve with chips, crackers, or raw vegetables. Yield: 1¾ cups.

GREEN GODDESS DIP

¾ cup commercial sour cream
¾ cup mayonnaise or salad
   dressing
1 (2-ounce) can anchovy
   fillets, drained and finely
   chopped

⅓ cup chopped parsley
3 tablespoons chopped chives
1 tablespoon vinegar
1 clove garlic, crushed
¼ teaspoon salt
⅛ teaspoon pepper

Combine all ingredients; cover and refrigerate overnight to mellow flavors. Yield: 2 cups.

GUACAMOLE DIP

1 small onion, finely chopped
1 small dried red pepper,
   finely chopped (optional)
1 medium tomato, finely
   chopped
6 peeled avocados, finely
   chopped

2½ teaspoons salt
2 teaspoons lemon juice
2 tablespoons mayonnaise
1 teaspoon salad oil
4 drops hot pepper sauce

Combine all ingredients in a large bowl. Serve as a dip or dressing. Yield: 5 to 6 cups.

DEVILED HAM DIP

1 (5-ounce) jar pimiento-
   cheese spread
1 (2¼-ounce) can deviled
   ham

½ cup mayonnaise or salad
   dressing
1 tablespoon minced onion
Few drops hot pepper sauce

Combine all ingredients; chill. Yield: about 1⅓ cups.

SOUR CREAM HAM DIP

1 (8-ounce) carton commercial
  sour cream
½ cup ground cooked ham
1¼ teaspoons dry sherry

1¼ teaspoons prepared
  mustard
¾ teaspoon instant minced
  onion

Combine all ingredients; chill until ready to serve. Yield: about 1½ cups.

HOT HAMBURGER DIP

1 pound lean ground beef
½ cup chopped onion
1 (8-ounce) can tomato sauce
¼ cup catsup
1 (8-ounce) package cream
  cheese

½ cup grated Parmesan
  cheese
1 clove garlic, minced
1 teaspoon oregano
1 teaspoon sugar
Salt and pepper to taste

Sauté ground beef until browned; add onion and cook until tender. Add remaining ingredients, and stir over low heat until cheese melts. Spoon into a chafing dish and keep warm; serve with corn chips. Yield: 4 cups.

Hot Hamburger Dip (above)

INDIA DIP

½ cup mayonnaise
1 tablespoon peach preserves

1 teaspoon Dijon mustard

Place all ingredients in a covered blender. Blend until smooth on medium speed. Good as a vegetable dip or a fruit salad dressing. Delightful on cold chicken, shrimp, ham, fish fingers, etc. Yield: about ½ cup.

LEMON PEPPER DIP

2 (8-ounce) cartons
  commercial sour cream
1 tablespoon plus 1 teaspoon
  commercial lemon pepper
  marinade

Raw vegetables

Blend sour cream and lemon pepper marinade. Refrigerate 1 to 2 hours before serving. Serve with assorted raw vegetables such as cherry tomatoes, carrots, cauliflower, fennel, celery, and broccoli. Yield: 2 cups.

LIPTAUER DIP

1 (8-ounce) package cream
  cheese, softened
½ cup butter or margarine,
  softened
1½ tablespoons anchovy
  paste, or 1 (¾-ounce) can
  anchovies, mashed with
  liquid
1½ tablespoons drained
  capers

1 teaspoon paprika
1 teaspoon caraway seed
½ teaspoon Dijon mustard
1 (8-ounce) carton commercial
  sour cream
Juice of 1 lemon
Raw vegetables, potato chips,
  or melba toast

Blend cream cheese and butter thoroughly. Stir in all other ingredients except raw vegetables until smooth. The flavor of this dip improves if allowed to mellow overnight in the refrigerator. Excellent as a dip for raw vegetables, potato chips, or as a spread for melba toast. Yield: about 3 cups.

▪ *Sometimes guests are reluctant to be the first to help themselves to a spectacular, edible table arrangement like grapefruit shells filled with strawberries, cantaloupe shells filled with green and pink melon balls, or other beautiful fruit. Conspire with a friend to wait until the crowd around the table is at its height, then have her casually spear a piece of the fruit with a cocktail pick. Once the trend is started, your fruit centerpiece will be enjoyed to the hilt.*

LOBSTER DUNK

2 tablespoons butter or
 margarine
2 tablespoons chopped onion
2 tablespoons chopped green
 pepper
½ cup half-and-half
1 tablespoon cornstarch
1 (10¾-ounce) can cream of
 mushroom soup, undiluted

2 egg yolks, slightly beaten
2 (5½-ounce) cans lobster
 meat, drained and cut into
 small pieces
2 tablespoons cooking sherry
⅛ teaspoon ground nutmeg
1 cup shredded Cheddar
 cheese
Crackers

Melt butter in a saucepan. Stir in onion and green pepper; sauté for 10 minutes. Blend half-and-half and cornstarch. Stir into soup and add egg yolks; blend into sautéed vegetables. Stir in lobster, sherry, and nutmeg. Heat, stirring constantly, until thickened. Add cheese. Stir until cheese is melted. Serve in a chafing dish with crackers. Yield: about 3½ cups.

LOBSTER FONDUE DIP

2 tablespoons butter or
 margarine
2 cups shredded sharp
 process American cheese
2 drops of hot pepper sauce

⅓ cup dry white wine
1 (5-ounce) can lobster,
 drained and broken into
 small pieces

Melt butter in a small saucepan. Gradually stir in cheese over low heat until cheese melts. (Cheese and butter mixture may appear separated at this point.) Add hot pepper sauce; slowly add wine, stirring until mixture is smooth. Add lobster; stir until heated through. Serve hot in a chafing dish. Yield: about 1½ cups.

WESTERN OLIVE DIP

1 (8-ounce) package cream
 cheese, softened
1 to 2 tablespoons commercial
 sour cream

1 teaspoon chili powder
1½ teaspoons grated onion
½ cup chopped ripe olives
Corn chips

Beat cheese with other ingredients except olives and corn chips in small bowl of electric mixer. When smooth and light, fold in olives. Chill thoroughly and serve with corn chips. Yield: about 1½ cups.

SMOKED OYSTER DIP

2 (8-ounce) packages cream
 cheese, softened
1 teaspoon Worcestershire
 sauce
2 teaspoons lemon juice

1 (8-ounce) carton commercial
 sour cream
1 (3⅔-ounce) can smoked
 oysters, undrained
Corn chips

Blend cheese with Worcestershire sauce, lemon juice, and sour cream. Combine with undrained oysters. Serve with corn chips. Yield: about 3 cups.

PARISIAN DIP

1 (8-ounce) package cream
  cheese, softened
1 (3-ounce) package Roquefort
  cheese
3 tablespoons half-and-half

1½ teaspoons chopped chives,
  divided
½ teaspoon Worcestershire
  sauce
Potato chips

Combine cream cheese, Roquefort cheese, half-and-half, 1 teaspoon chives, and Worcestershire sauce. Mix until well blended. Sprinkle with remaining chives. Serve with potato chips. Yield: about 1½ cups.

ANCHOVY SAUCE FOR SEAFOOD

1 tablespoon anchovy paste
1 tablespoon paprika
Pinch of salt, if needed
2 tablespoons tarragon vinegar

1 cup mayonnaise
½ cup whipping cream,
  whipped

Mix anchovy paste, paprika, salt, and vinegar. Gradually blend into mayonnaise, mixing well after each addition. Fold in cream. If mixture is too thick, thin with a little cream. Yield: 2 cups.

COCKTAIL SAUCE FOR SHRIMP

2 cups catsup or chili sauce
½ cup Worcestershire sauce
½ cup minced celery
½ cup chopped fresh parsley
¼ cup prepared horseradish

¼ cup lemon juice
Dash of hot pepper sauce
Dash of sugar
Salt to taste

Combine all ingredients the day before using. This yields enough sauce for 5 pounds raw shrimp in the shell. Yield: about 4 cups.

TANGY DIP SAUCE FOR HOT HORS D'OEUVRES

½ cup chili sauce
⅓ cup catsup
3 tablespoons prepared
  horseradish

1½ teaspoons Worcestershire
  sauce

Combine chili sauce, catsup, horseradish, and Worcestershire sauce. Mix well. Yield: about ¾ cup.

SHRIMP DIP

1 (8-ounce) package cream
  cheese
⅓ cup commercial sour cream
2 teaspoons lemon juice
¼ teaspoon onion juice

Dash of Worcestershire sauce
1 cup chopped cooked shrimp
Paprika
Potato chips

Soften cheese and blend in sour cream and seasonings. Stir in shrimp and add paprika as desired for color. Serve with sturdy potato chips or other "dippers." Yield: 2½ cups.

CREAMY SHRIMP DIP

2 (8-ounce) packages cream
  cheese, softened
1 (3-ounce) package cream
  cheese with chives
1 (10¾-ounce) can cream of
  shrimp soup, undiluted
1½ cups chopped cooked
  shrimp
1 teaspoon dry mustard
1 teaspoon Worcestershire
  sauce

¼ teaspoon garlic powder
½ to 1 teaspoon paprika
Salt and pepper to taste
¾ to 1 cup mayonnaise
1 cup drained, cooked
  crabmeat (optional)

Combine ingredients in a large bowl at least 2 hours before serving. Chill. Yield: about 6½ cups.

SHRIMP CHIP DIP

1 (4½-ounce) can shrimp
1 (8-ounce) carton commercial
  sour cream
¼ cup chili sauce
2 teaspoons lemon juice

½ teaspoon salt
⅛ teaspoon pepper
1 teaspoon prepared
  horseradish
Dash of hot pepper sauce

Cut shrimp into very small pieces and mix well with other ingredients. Chill. Yield: 1½ cups.

ZESTY SHRIMP DIP

½ pound fresh cooked shrimp,
  or 1 (5-ounce) can shrimp
1 (8-ounce) carton creamy
  cottage cheese
3 tablespoons chili sauce
½ teaspoon onion juice

½ teaspoon lemon juice
¼ teaspoon Worcestershire
  sauce
¼ cup milk
Potato chips, crackers, and
  celery

Finely chop shrimp and add to cottage cheese. Stir in chili sauce, onion juice, lemon juice, and Worcestershire sauce. Gradually beat in enough milk to give good dipping consistency. Serve with potato chips, crackers, and celery. Yield: about 2 cups.

Dill Dip for Raw Vegetables (page 97)

TALLAHASSEE SHRIMP DIP

½ pound cooked, peeled
   shrimp, fresh or frozen
1 (1⅜-ounce) package dry
   onion soup mix
2 (8-ounce) cartons
   commercial sour cream

¼ cup catsup
1 tablespoon chopped parsley
Assorted crackers

Thaw frozen shrimp. Chop shrimp. Combine all ingredients except crack-ers. Mix thoroughly. Chill. Serve with crackers. Yield: about 3¼ cups.

SKINNY DIP

½ cup watercress, stems and
   leaves included
3 tablespoons skim milk
1 cup diced green pepper
1 cup low-fat cottage cheese

12 stuffed green olives
⅛ teaspoon pepper
Dash of hot pepper sauce
Dash of salt
Raw vegetables

Wash and dry watercress. Blend all ingredients except raw vegetables on high speed of blender until smooth. Chill. Serve with raw vegetables such as carrot sticks, celery, radishes, cauliflower, etc. Yield: about 2¼ cups.

CREAMY SPINACH-DILL DIP

1 (8-ounce) carton commercial
   sour cream
1 cup mayonnaise
½ cup chopped green onion
½ cup chopped parsley

1 tablespoon dillweed
1 teaspoon Ac'cent
¾ to 1 teaspoon salt
1 (10-ounce) package frozen
   spinach, thawed

Combine all ingredients in container of electric blender; process on high speed 1 to 2 minutes or until smooth and creamy. Chill mixture overnight. Serve with crisp, raw vegetables. Yield: about 3 cups.

SUMMERTIME DIP

1 cup mayonnaise
¼ cup chili sauce
¼ cup catsup
1 medium onion, grated
2 cloves garlic, minced

1½ teaspoons dry mustard
1 teaspoon pepper
Dash of paprika
Dash of hot sauce

Combine all ingredients in a jar; shake well. Chill 3 to 4 hours. Serve with cold boiled shrimp and assorted raw vegetables. Yield: about 2 cups.
   Note: May be served as salad dressing. Add ¼ cup salad oil to jar; shake well, and chill.

TOMATO AND GREEN ONION DIP

1 medium tomato, chopped
½ cup lemon juice
½ teaspoon salt
½ teaspoon pepper
¼ cup minced green onions
2 (8-ounce) cartons
   commercial sour cream

¼ teaspoon Worcestershire
   sauce
½ teaspoon sugar
Raw vegetables

Marinate tomato in lemon juice, salt, and pepper for 1 hour. Blend with remaining ingredients except vegetables. Serve as a dip for raw vegetables. Yield: about 3 cups.

TAPENADE DIP

1 (6½-ounce) can white
   solid-pack tuna, drained
2 anchovy fillets
1 tablespoon anchovy oil
¼ cup chopped ripe olives
½ small onion, grated
1 clove garlic, crushed
¼ cup chopped celery

¼ cup cubed cooked potato
½ teaspoon Worcestershire
   sauce
Dash of hot pepper sauce
Juice of 1 small lemon
Pepper
½ cup mayonnaise
Raw vegetables

Blend all ingredients except raw vegetables in blender until smooth. Use as a dip for raw vegetables. Yield: about 2 cups.

Note: The average home electric blender resists blending such solid matter as the above; you must use a rubber spatula to repeatedly push the mixture into the path of the blades. You might find it easier to do half the recipe at a time. This is an excellent, different hors d'oeuvre, well worth the trouble to prepare. Don't omit the potatoes; they contribute to the smooth texture.

TUNA CREAM DIP

1 (6½- or 7-ounce) can tuna,
   drained and flaked
1 tablespoon prepared
   horseradish
1½ teaspoons onion salt
1 teaspoon Worcestershire
   sauce

1 (8-ounce) carton commercial
   sour cream
2 teaspoons chopped parsley
Potato chips

Combine tuna, horseradish, onion salt, and Worcestershire sauce; fold in sour cream. Chill. Garnish with parsley and serve with potato chips. Yield: about 1½ cups.

TUNA PARTY DIP

2 (6½- or 7-ounce) cans tuna
  in vegetable oil
2 (8-ounce) cartons
  commercial sour cream

1 (1⅜-ounce) package dry
  onion soup mix
1 teaspoon hot pepper sauce
Crackers or potato chips

Combine first 4 ingredients; chill. Serve with crackers or potato chips. Yield: about 3½ cups.

TUNA PINEAPPLE DIP

1 (8¼-ounce) can crushed
  pineapple
1 (6½- or 7-ounce) can tuna,
  drained and flaked
1 (8-ounce) package cream
  cheese, softened

3 tablespoons pineapple juice
Dash of salt
Dash of ground nutmeg

Drain pineapple and reserve liquid. Combine all ingredients; blend into a paste. Chill. Yield: about 2 cups.

VEGETABLE CHIP DIP

1 tablespoon mayonnaise
1 tablespoon crumbled blue
  cheese
1 tablespoon chopped
  watercress
1½ cups cooked asparagus
  tips

1 hard-cooked egg, chopped
½ teaspoon salt
Pinch of pepper
Potato chips

Combine first 7 ingredients. Chill. Serve with potato chips. Yield: about 2 cups.

CURRY SAUCE FOR RAW VEGETABLES

½ cup mayonnaise
1 (8-ounce) carton commercial
  sour cream
2 tablespoons lemon juice
Salt and pepper to taste
1 teaspoon curry powder
½ teaspoon paprika
2 tablespoons minced fresh
  parsley

½ teaspoon tarragon
2 tablespoons grated onion
2 teaspoons prepared mustard
1 tablespoon minced chives
Several dashes of hot pepper
  sauce
Raw vegetables

Combine mayonnaise, sour cream, and lemon juice. Blend with all other ingredients except vegetables. Check seasonings and chill overnight before serving. Use as a dip for an assortment of raw vegetables (cauliflower flowerets, sliced raw yellow squash, cucumber slices, celery sticks, carrot sticks, etc.). Yield: about 2 cups.

MALLEY'S DIP FOR RAW VEGETABLES

2 cups mayonnaise
2 (8-ounce) cartons
  commercial sour cream
3 tablespoons minced fresh
  parsley or 1 tablespoon
  dried parsley

3 tablespoons grated onion
3 tablespoons dillweed
1½ tablespoons seasoned salt

Blend all ingredients together and chill before serving. May be made several days ahead of time. Yield: about 4½ cups.

RAW VEGETABLES WITH HERB SAUCE

1 (8-ounce) carton commercial
  sour cream
1 (8-ounce) package cream
  cheese, softened
1 tablespoon minced chives
1 tablespoon minced fresh
  parsley

2 teaspoons soy sauce
1 teaspoon tarragon
1 teaspoon dillweed
1 teaspoon curry powder
Milk
Raw vegetables

Blend sour cream into softened cheese. Add all other ingredients except vegetables, using enough milk to yield a dipping consistency. Blend thoroughly. May be prepared a day or so ahead of time. Serve with raw vegetables. Yield: about 2 cups.

APRICOT-ALMOND FILLING

1 cup stewed dried apricots
½ cup chopped almonds

1 tablespoon grated orange
  rind

Combine all ingredients and mix well. Yield: about 1½ cups.

SIMPLE AVOCADO SPREAD

2 avocados
1 tablespoon lemon juice
1 teaspoon salt
¼ teaspoon Worcestershire
  sauce

Cottage cheese, cream cheese,
  or mayonnaise (optional)

Cut each avocado into halves and remove seed and skin. Force avocado through sieve or simply mash well with fork. Blend in remaining ingredients. (Cottage cheese, cream cheese, or mayonnaise may be mixed with spread to make the avocado go further.) Yield: about 1 cup.

BLACK BEAN CRACKER SPREAD

1 (11-ounce) can black bean
  soup, undiluted
1 (8-ounce) can tomato sauce
½ to 1 cup shredded sharp
  Cheddar cheese, divided

¼ teaspoon chili powder
Crackers or corn chips

Combine black bean soup, tomato sauce, ½ cup cheese, and chili powder; cook over medium heat until cheese melts. Add more cheese until spread is as thick as desired. Serve warm as a spread for crackers or as a dip for chips. Yield: about 2½ cups.

BRAUNSCHWEIGER MOLD

½ pound braunschweiger
  (liver sausage), chopped
1 (3-ounce) package cream
  cheese, softened
¼ cup mayonnaise
1 to 2 tablespoons
  half-and-half
1 tablespoon melted butter or
  margarine

1 tablespoon dry sherry
½ teaspoon curry powder
¼ teaspoon salt
¼ teaspoon black pepper
Pinch of cayenne pepper
Pinch of ground nutmeg
1 tablespoon Worcestershire
  sauce
Rye bread rounds

Beat sausage, cream cheese, mayonnaise, and half-and-half in small bowl of an electric mixer. When blended, beat in remaining ingredients except rye bread rounds; turn into lightly oiled mold or bowl in which spread is to be served. Chill until ready to serve. (May be made day before serving.) Surround bowl with small rounds of rye bread. Yield: about 2 cups.

▪ *Make ice cubes ahead of time and store them in plastic bags in the freezer. Count on 350 cubes for 50 people, or seven cubes per person.*

▪ *Use insulated ice chests to keep bottled drinks and other items cold. This saves refrigerator space.*

Braunschweiger Spread (below); Cheesy Pimiento Spread (page 126); Shrimp Spread (page 139); Fresh Vegetable Spread (page 139)

Spreads & Fillings

BRAUNSCHWEIGER SPREAD

½ cup finely chopped fresh
   mushrooms
1 tablespoon melted butter
2 (4-ounce) rolls
   braunschweiger, softened

2 tablespoons mayonnaise
½ teaspoon Worcestershire
   sauce
Salt to taste

Sauté mushrooms in butter just until tender or about 1 to 2 minutes. Remove from heat, and add remaining ingredients; mix well. Yield: about 1½ cups.

CANAPÉ SPREAD

1 (8-ounce) package cream
   cheese, softened
¼ cup mayonnaise
1 teaspoon prepared mustard
1 teaspoon Worcestershire
   sauce
Few drops of hot pepper sauce

1 teaspoon prepared
   horseradish
1 hard-cooked egg, minced
2 tablespoons minced stuffed
   olives
1 (4½-ounce) can deviled
   ham

Combine cream cheese, mayonnaise, mustard, Worcestershire sauce, and hot pepper sauce; whip until fluffy. Blend in other ingredients and chill. Yield: about 2 cups.

SEAFOOD CANAPÉ SPREAD

1 (3-ounce) package cream
   cheese, softened
½ cup butter or margarine,
   softened
½ cup cottage cheese
2 teaspoons anchovy paste
1 teaspoon caraway seed,
   crushed (optional)

1 teaspoon dry mustard
1 teaspoon paprika
1 teaspoon grated onion
Sandwich bread slices
Pimiento
Parsley
Anchovy, shrimp, or sardines
   (optional)

Beat together cream cheese, butter, cottage cheese, anchovy paste, caraway seed (if desired), mustard, paprika, and onion in small mixing bowl. Cover and chill to blend flavors. Serve at room temperature as a spread. To make canapés, remove crust from slices of sandwich bread. Cover each slice with spread. Garnish with pimiento and parsley. Cut in two. Place anchovy, shrimp, or sardine fillet on each, if desired. Yield: 1½ cups.

AMSTERDAM CHEESE MOLD

1 (about 8 ounces) small
   round Gouda cheese
2 ounces crumbled blue
   cheese
½ cup commercial sour cream

¼ cup butter or margarine
2 tablespoons wine vinegar or
   cider vinegar
1 tablespoon grated onion
⅛ teaspoon cayenne pepper

Peel the rind from Gouda cheese and shred cheese into a saucepan. Add all other ingredients and heat slowly, stirring constantly with a wooden spoon until cheeses melt completely and mixture is smooth. (If you have an electric blender, use it for a more velvety texture after cheeses are completely melted.) Lightly oil a 2-cup mold and pour in cheese. Cover and chill overnight. When ready to serve, unmold by running a sharp knife around mold and shaking it onto a serving plate. This is best served at room temperature, as the flavor is delicate and serving it ice-cold tends to detract from the subtlety. Yield: about 1½ cups.

ANCHOVY CHEESE

1 (16-ounce) carton cottage
   cheese
4 drained anchovies, finely
   shredded, oil reserved
2 tablespoons chopped fresh
   parsley
2 tablespoons minced chives
   or onion
1 teaspoon poppy seed (do not
   omit)

About 1 teaspoon lemon juice
About ½ teaspoon oil drained
   from anchovies
Salt to taste
Pumpernickel, melba toast, or
   dark rye bread rounds

Combine all ingredients except salt, pumpernickel, melba toast, and rye bread rounds, in a bowl; taste and add salt if needed. (The anchovies lend a good bit of salt to the mixture.) Mound the cheese in center of a serving dish; surround with pumpernickel, melba toast, or dark rye bread rounds. Yield: about 2 cups.

APPETIZER CHEESE MOUSSE

2 teaspoons unflavored gelatin
¼ cup cold water
2 cups commercial sour cream
2 teaspoons Italian salad
   dressing mix

¼ cup crumbled blue cheese
1 cup cream-style cottage
   cheese
Parsley
Carrot curls

Soften gelatin in cold water. Place over boiling water and stir until gelatin dissolves. Stir dissolved gelatin into sour cream. Add salad dressing mix, blue cheese, and cottage cheese; beat with electric mixer or rotary beater until well blended. Pour into a 3½-cup ring mold. Chill until firm. Unmold and garnish with parsley and carrot curls. Yield: about 3 cups.

PARTY CHEESE MOUSSE

2 envelopes unflavored gelatin
1½ cups beef broth
1 large clove garlic, pressed
¼ teaspoon curry powder
Salt and pepper to taste

4 (3-ounce) packages cream
   cheese, softened
Pimiento strips
Parsley
Crackers

Sprinkle gelatin over beef broth in a saucepan; let stand until softened. Place over medium heat, stirring until gelatin is dissolved; cool completely.

Combine gelatin mixture, garlic, curry powder, salt, and pepper in container of electric blender; blend 30 seconds. Cube cream cheese; add a small amount at a time to blender, blending until smooth.

Pour mixture into a 3-cup mold. Refrigerate until firm, at least 3 hours. Unmold; garnish with pimiento and parsley. Serve with crackers. Yield: 3 cups.

Photograph for this recipe on page 154

BRANDIED CHEDDAR CHEESE

4 cups shredded sharp
   Cheddar cheese
2 tablespoons butter or
   margarine

1 teaspoon sugar
Dash of cayenne pepper
½ cup brandy, divided
Crackers

Have cheese and butter at room temperature. Add sugar, cayenne pepper, and ¼ cup brandy; mix by hand or beat with electric mixer until quite smooth. Gradually add remaining ¼ cup brandy, mixing until creamy. Store in covered crock in refrigerator. Keeps indefinitely. Serve at room temperature with crackers. Yield: about 2 cups.

Spreads & Fillings

CHEDDAR BLUE MOLD

2 cups shredded Cheddar
  cheese
1 (8-ounce) package cream
  cheese, softened
8 ounces blue cheese,
  crumbled

½ cup lemon soda
¼ teaspoon hot pepper sauce
¼ teaspoon Worcestershire
  sauce
1 teaspoon dry mustard
Crackers

Blend all ingredients except crackers. Pack into a 3-cup mold. Chill thoroughly. Unmold; serve with assorted crackers. Yield: 3 cups.

BLUE CHEESE BALL

1 (8-ounce) package cream
  cheese, softened
¼ cup crumbled blue cheese

1 tablespoon grated onion
½ cup chopped parsley

Beat cream cheese, blue cheese, and onion until smooth. Chill for ease in handling. Shape into a ball; wrap in waxed paper. Chill. Just before serving, roll in chopped parsley. Yield: 1¼ cups.

CHEESE BALL

6 (3-ounce) packages cream
  cheese, softened
½ pound sharp cheese
2 teaspoons grated onion
2 teaspoons Worcestershire
  sauce

2 teaspoons finely minced
  garlic (dried onion flakes
  and garlic powder may be
  substituted)
Finely chopped nuts (pecan or
  peanut)

Put all ingredients except nuts in the large bowl of an electric mixer and blend well. Refrigerate until firm; shape into a ball. Roll in chopped nuts until well coated. Wrap in plastic or heavy-duty aluminum foil and let ripen in refrigerator for at least 24 hours. Remove from refrigerator at least 2 hours before serving. Yield: about 3 cups.

CHRISTMAS-GREEN CHEESE BALL

1 (¼-pound) wedge natural
  blue cheese, crumbled
1 tablespoon minced celery
2 or 3 scallions or green
  onions, including tops,
  finely chopped
2 tablespoons commercial
  sour cream

3 (5-ounce) jars blue cheese
  spread
1 cup coarsely chopped
  parsley

Combine blue cheese, celery, scallions, sour cream, and blue cheese spread until fluffy; mix on medium speed of electric mixer. Shape into a ball, wrap in heavy-duty aluminum foil, and refrigerate overnight.

At serving time, remove foil and reshape into a ball; roll in parsley until completely coated. Yield: about 1½ cups.

CHRISTMAS-RED CHEESE BALL

2 cups shredded natural Cheddar cheese	Dash of onion salt
1 (3-ounce) package cream cheese, softened	Dash of celery salt
	Dash of garlic salt
3 tablespoons sherry	½ teaspoon Worcestershire sauce
¼ cup coarsely chopped pitted ripe olives	½ cup coarsely chopped dried beef

Combine cheeses, sherry, olives, salts, and Worcestershire sauce; mix on medium speed of electric mixer. Shape mixture into a ball; wrap in heavy-duty aluminum foil; refrigerate overnight or until needed.

About 30 minutes before serving time, remove foil; reshape into a ball; roll ball in dried beef, coating well. Yield: about 1½ cups.

EASY CHEESE BALL

2 cups shredded sharp Cheddar cheese	2 teaspoons grated onion
1 (8-ounce) package cream cheese	Cayenne pepper to taste
	1 teaspoon Worcestershire sauce
¼ pound Roquefort or blue cheese	1 cup finely minced parsley
1 clove garlic, crushed	1 cup chopped pecans

Thoroughly mix all ingredients except parsley and pecans. Combine parsley and pecans; blend half of parsley mixture into cheese mixture. Spread remaining parsley mixture on sheet of waxed paper. Form cheese into a ball and roll it in parsley mixture until well coated. Chill before serving. May be made long before serving. Freezes beautifully. Yield: about 2½ cups.

115

GINGER BALL

3 (8-ounce) packages cream
    cheese, softened
2 (2-ounce) jars crystallized
    ginger

2 or more teaspoons ground
    ginger
1 cup finely chopped pecans
Crackers or vegetables

Combine cream cheese and ginger until thoroughly blended. Shape into a ball and store in refrigerator at least 24 hours before serving. About half an hour before serving, roll ball in chopped pecans and allow to come to room temperature. Serve with crackers or with crisp vegetable wedges. Yield: about 3 cups.

GOURMET CHEESE BALL

3 (8-ounce) packages cream
    cheese, softened
1 cup drained and chopped
    preserved ginger

¾ cup canned diced roasted
    buttered almonds

Combine cheese and ginger; mix until well blended. Shape into a ball, wrap in heavy-duty aluminum foil, and refrigerate overnight.

At serving time, remove foil and reshape into a ball; roll in almonds until completely coated. Yield: 3 cups.

PARTY CHEESE BALL

2 (8-ounce) packages cream
    cheese, softened
2 cups shredded sharp natural
    Cheddar cheese
1 tablespoon chopped
    pimiento
1 tablespoon chopped green
    pepper

1 tablespoon finely chopped
    onion
2 teaspoons Worcestershire
    sauce
1 teaspoon lemon juice
Dash of cayenne pepper
Dash of salt
Finely chopped pecans

Combine softened cream cheese and Cheddar cheese, mixing until well blended. Add pimiento, green pepper, onion, Worcestershire sauce, lemon juice, and seasonings; mix well. Chill. Shape into a ball and roll in chopped pecans. Yield: 3 cups.

• *To get maximum volume when beating egg whites, have them at room temperature and beat in a deep glass or metal bowl—not plastic. Tip the bowl to determine if whites have reached the proper consistency. The whites will not slide when they've reached the "stiff but not dry" stage called for in many recipes.*

116

PINEAPPLE CHEESE BALL

2 (8-ounce) packages cream
  cheese, softened
1 (8½-ounce) can crushed
  pineapple, drained
¼ cup finely chopped green
  pepper

2 tablespoons chopped onion
1 tablespoon seasoned salt
2 cups chopped pecans,
  divided
Crackers

Combine first 5 ingredients; add 1 cup pecans, and mix well. Refrigerate until firm, and shape into a ball. Roll in remaining pecans before serving. Garnish as desired. Serve with an assortment of crackers. Yield: about 3 cups.

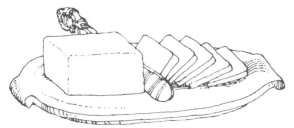

SNOWMAN CHEESE BALL

2 (8-ounce) packages cream
  cheese, softened
2 cups crumbled Roquefort
  cheese
2 tablespoons grated onion
1½ teaspoons prepared
  mustard

1 tablespoon Worcestershire
  sauce
⅛ teaspoon cayenne pepper
3 or 4 stuffed olives
1 strip pimiento
1 tablespoon seedless raisins

Combine cheeses, onion, mustard, Worcestershire sauce, and cayenne pepper; mix until smooth. Cover and chill for 30 minutes or until firm enough to shape. Shape into 3 balls using 1½ cups for first, 1 cup for second, and ½ cup for third. Arrange one on top of another to form a snowman. Slice olives for eyes and nose; use pimiento strip for mouth and olive slices for buttons. Put raisins on toothpicks and insert as arms. Cut hat from cardboard and cover with foil. Yield: 3 cups.

Note: Mixture may be shaped into a single ball and dusted with paprika or rolled in ground pecans.

• *When buying liquor, remember that there are seventeen 1½-ounce drinks in a fifth of liquor (about 200 drinks to a case). For easy calculation, plan three drinks per guest. Although some guests will have only one drink, it's better to have too much than not enough. Provide a large pitcher of chilled fruit juice and an assortment of carbonated drinks for nondrinkers. Have a tray or table handy for used glasses.*

Special Cheese Ball (below)

SPECIAL CHEESE BALL

2 (8-ounce) packages cream
   cheese
1 pound sharp Cheddar cheese
1 pound mild natural Cheddar
   cheese
1 pound process cheese
   spread
1 tablespoon Worcestershire
   sauce

1 medium onion, finely
   chopped
Chopped nuts, chili powder, or
   minced parsley
Parsley sprigs (optional)
Crackers

Let cheeses reach room temperature. Using an electric blender or heavy-duty mixer, blend cheeses until smooth and creamy. Add Worcestershire sauce and onion; mix well. Chill.

Shape into 2 balls, and roll each in nuts, chili powder, or minced parsley; chill. Garnish with parsley, if desired. Serve with crackers. Yield: two 2½-pound cheese balls.

TRIO CHEESE BALL

1 (8-ounce) package cream
   cheese, softened
¼ pound blue cheese,
   crumbled
1 cup shredded sharp Cheddar
   cheese

1 small onion, minced
1 tablespoon Worcestershire
   sauce
½ cup chopped pecans
Finely chopped parsley
Small crisp crackers

Beat cheeses on medium speed of electric mixer until fluffy, scraping sides and bottom of bowl often. Beat in onion and Worcestershire sauce. Stir in pecans. Cover and chill for 3 to 4 hours. Mold cheese mixture into one large ball or into 30 to 36 small balls, each about 1 inch in diameter; roll in parsley. Cover and chill until firm, about 2 hours. Arrange a variety of crackers on a plate around cheese ball; serve as a spread, or insert colored wooden picks in center of small balls and serve with crackers. Yield: 2½ cups.

VERSATILE CHEESE BALL

2 cups shredded Cheddar
   cheese
1 cup crumbled blue cheese
½ cup shredded provolone
   cheese
1 (3-ounce) package cream
   cheese, softened
1 tablespoon milk
1 tablespoon grated onion

1 teaspoon Worcestershire
   sauce
½ teaspoon dry mustard
½ teaspoon paprika
¼ teaspoon garlic salt
¼ teaspoon celery salt
¼ cup toasted sesame seed

Beat Cheddar, blue, provolone, and cream cheeses until smooth. Blend in milk, onion, Worcestershire sauce, mustard, paprika, and garlic and celery salts. Chill for ease in handling. Shape into a ball; roll in sesame seed. Wrap in waxed paper; chill. Yield: 2 cups.

ZESTY CHEESE BALL

1 pound Cheddar cheese,
   softened
1 (8-ounce) package cream
   cheese, softened
Dash of onion salt or juice
Dash of garlic salt

Dash of hot pepper sauce
Dash of Worcestershire sauce
Dash of salt
½ cup chopped nuts, toasted
Paprika

Blend softened cheeses. Add seasonings to taste; blend well. Shape cheese into a ball and roll in nuts. (Chill cheese slightly in order to roll more easily.) Sprinkle ball with paprika. Yield: 3 cups.

WALNUT CHEESE BALL

1 cup shredded natural
  Cheddar cheese
1 (3-ounce) package cream
  cheese, softened
¼ pound blue cheese,
  crumbled

1 tablespoon prepared mustard
3 tablespoons cooking sherry
1 teaspoon grated onion
¼ teaspoon hot pepper sauce
1 cup walnuts, chopped

Combine all ingredients except walnuts. Shape into a ball. Roll in chopped walnuts, coating surface thickly. Wrap in heavy-duty aluminum foil and chill 24 hours. Can be kept about a week if refrigerated. Yield: about 1½ cups.

STUFFED EDAM CHEESE

1 (8-ounce) round Edam
  cheese
¼ cup sherry
½ teaspoon prepared mustard
½ teaspoon Worcestershire
  sauce

⅛ teaspoon salt
⅛ teaspoon onion salt
⅛ teaspoon garlic salt
⅛ teaspoon cayenne pepper

Remove a 3-inch circle from top of cheese; scoop out inside. Crumble cheese and measure it tightly packed. (Measurements for wine and seasonings are for 1 cup cheese. Increase amounts for a larger Edam.) Blend wine and seasonings into cheese. Pack mixture into cheese shell; replace top. Chill. Bring to room temperature to serve. Yield: 6 to 8 servings.

GOUDA PARTY SCOOP

1 (8-ounce) round Gouda
  cheese
½ teaspoon prepared mustard
½ teaspoon Worcestershire
  sauce

⅛ teaspoon salt
⅛ teaspoon onion salt
⅛ teaspoon garlic salt

Bring cheese to room temperature. Using scalloped cookie cutter, cut wax from top of cheese. Carefully remove cheese from shell; keep shell intact. Beat cheese until smooth; add remaining ingredients and beat until well blended. Refill shell. Yield: about 1 cup.

CHEESE LOG

1 (8-ounce) package cream
  cheese, softened
1 (4-ounce) roll bacon and
  horseradish cheese spread
1 (1⅜-ounce) package dry
  onion soup mix

1 teaspoon chili powder
¼ teaspoon garlic powder
½ cup chopped peanuts
Rye bread

Blend all ingredients except peanuts and rye bread. Shape into a 10- x 2½-inch roll; wrap in waxed paper and chill for 4 hours. Remove paper, roll in peanuts, and serve with rye bread. Yield: 1½ cups.

BACON CHEESE LOGS

1 pound bacon
1 (8-ounce) package cream
   cheese, softened
½ cup chopped pecans
¼ teaspoon garlic salt

¼ teaspoon Worcestershire
   sauce
4 drops hot pepper sauce
1 tablespoon chili powder
Crackers

Cook bacon until crisp; drain and crumble. Blend with remaining ingredients except chili powder and crackers. Shape into 2 rolls about 1 inch in diameter. Sprinkle chili powder on waxed paper; roll logs in chili powder to coat evenly. Wrap tightly in waxed paper. Chill. Slice and serve on crackers. Yield: about 5 dozen.

CARAWAY CHEESE LOG

1 (8-ounce) package cream
   cheese, softened
⅓ cup white wine
1 tablespoon caraway seed
2 cups shredded Monterey
   Jack cheese

½ cup grated Parmesan
   cheese
Crackers

Beat cream cheese until fluffy. Blend in wine. Mix in caraway seed and Monterey Jack cheese. Sprinkle a layer of Parmesan cheese on waxed paper. Place ¼ of cheese mixture on Parmesan layer. Shape cheese, with hands, into a small log about 4 inches long and 1 inch wide, patting log with Parmesan cheese while shaping. Form 3 more logs. Chill for 1 hour or until firm enough to slice. Serve with crackers. Yield: 4 logs.

CHEDDAR CHEESE LOG

1 pound Cheddar cheese
1 tablespoon grated onion
1 teaspoon Worcestershire
   sauce

½ teaspoon paprika
½ cup chopped nuts

Cut cheese into small pieces and allow to come to room temperature. Beat cheese until smooth and creamy; add onion, Worcestershire sauce, and paprika and continue to beat until thoroughly blended. Shape into a roll 6 inches long and 2½ inches in diameter. Roll in nuts. Yield: 2 cups.

PECAN-CHEESE LOGS

2 (10-ounce) packages mild
  Cheddar cheese, shredded
  and softened
1 (8-ounce) package cream
  cheese, softened
¼ cup margarine, softened
1½ cups toasted chopped
  pecans, divided

2 tablespoons chopped green
  olives
2 tablespoons chopped
  pimiento
2 tablespoons grated onion

Combine cheeses and margarine, mixing until smooth. Add ¾ cup pecans
and remaining ingredients; chill slightly. Shape into four 6-inch logs, and
roll each in remaining pecans. Refrigerate until ready to serve. Yield:
about 1½ pounds.

GOURMET CHEESE RING

⅔ cup chopped walnuts or
  pecans, divided
1 (3-ounce) package cream
  cheese
1½ cups finely shredded
  Swiss cheese
1½ cups finely shredded
  Cheddar cheese

1½ ounces Roquefort cheese,
  crumbled
2 tablespoons commercial
  sour cream
⅛ teaspoon cayenne pepper

Have all ingredients at room temperature. Lightly grease a 3-cup ring
mold; coat with 2 tablespoons nuts. Blend the four cheeses with an electric
mixer until smooth and light. Stir in sour cream, cayenne pepper, and
remaining nuts. Pack into the mold. Refrigerate overnight. Unmold.
Allow to stand at room temperature ½ hour before serving. Yield: 2½
cups.

APPETIZER CHEESE ROLL

2 (3-ounce) packages cream
  cheese
2 cups shredded Cheddar
  cheese

⅓ cup crumbled blue cheese
Chopped parsley

Bring cheeses to room temperature. Beat together cream, Cheddar, and
blue cheeses until smooth. Chill for ease in handling. Shape into a roll 8
inches long. Roll in parsley. Chill until ready to serve. Yield: about 3 cups.

GARLIC CHEESE ROLL

4 cups shredded sharp
  Cheddar cheese
1 (8-ounce) package cream
  cheese
½ teaspoon salt
2 cloves garlic, crushed
3 dashes of hot pepper sauce

1 tablespoon Worcestershire
  sauce
1 tablespoon mayonnaise
¼ teaspoon dry mustard
2 tablespoons paprika
2 tablespoons chili powder

Blend the two cheeses in the large bowl of an electric mixer. Add all other ingredients, except paprika and chili powder, mixing until smooth. Mix paprika and chili powder together and spread evenly on a piece of waxed paper placed on a flat surface. Dust hands lightly with flour and shape cheese mixture into two rolls about the diameter of a silver dollar. Roll in paprika and chili powder until completely covered. Flatten ends of roll and coat them also. Wrap in waxed paper and refrigerate 24 hours before using. This cheese freezes (and refreezes!) beautifully. Yield: 3 cups.

LONDON CHEESE ROLL

1 (8-ounce) package cream
  cheese
1 (3-ounce) package cream
  cheese
1 (4-ounce) package blue
  cheese, crumbled

1 cup sliced ripe olives
2 cups coarsely chopped
  walnuts or pecans, divided
Crackers or melba rounds

Have cheeses at room temperature. Blend thoroughly in large bowl of electric mixer. Stir in olives and 1 cup nuts. Spread remaining nuts on a sheet of waxed paper. Flour hands lightly and shape mixture into long roll or 2 short rolls about the size of a silver dollar. Roll back and forth in nuts until well coated; wrap in waxed paper and refrigerate overnight before using. Serve with crackers or melba rounds. This cheese freezes beautifully and may be made well in advance of serving. Yield: about 2 cups.

ALOHA CHEESE SPREAD

1 (8-ounce) package cream
  cheese, softened
3 ounces blue cheese,
  crumbled
⅓ cup crushed pineapple,
  drained

⅓ cup chopped pecans
½ teaspoon ground ginger
Parsley
Chopped pimiento

Blend cheeses. Stir in pineapple, pecans, and ginger; mix well. Chill. Garnish with parsley and pimiento. Yield: 2 cups.

BLUE CHEESE WHIP

1 cup crumbled blue cheese
2 (8-ounce) cartons
commercial sour cream,
divided

Crackers, breadsticks, or raw
vegetables

Beat together cheese and ¼ cup sour cream; fold in remaining sour cream. Cover and chill. Serve as a spread for crackers, as a dip for breadsticks and raw vegetables, or as a filling for celery sticks. Yield: about 2 cups.

MOLDED BLUE CHEESE SPREAD .

⅔ cup minced fresh parsley
2 (3-ounce) packages cream
cheese, softened
1 (4-ounce) package blue
cheese, crumbled
1 teaspoon Worcestershire
sauce

Dash of cayenne pepper
1 tablespoon lemon juice
¼ cup mayonnaise
Unsalted crackers or melba
rounds

Prepare small mold by generously oiling the inside. Press parsley around sides and bottom.

Thoroughly combine cream cheese, blue cheese, Worcestershire sauce, cayenne pepper, and lemon juice in small bowl of electric mixer. Stir in mayonnaise until blended. Spoon carefully into prepared mold, cover, and chill. Unmold and serve with unsalted crackers or melba rounds. Yield: about 1¼ cups.

CREAMY CHEESE SPREAD

4 cups shredded Cheddar
cheese
1 (3-ounce) package cream
cheese, softened
½ cup chopped nuts

1 clove garlic, minced
Chili powder
Chopped parsley
Chopped nuts

Combine cheeses, ½ cup nuts, and garlic in a mixing bowl; knead until well blended. Divide into 3 equal parts, shaping each into a roll or ball. Coat 1 ball with chili powder, 1 with parsley, and 1 with nuts. Chill before serving. Keep refrigerated. Yield: about 3 cups.

DUTCH CHEESE SPREAD

1 (7-ounce) round Gouda or
Edam cheese, finely
shredded
½ cup commercial sour cream
¼ cup milk

½ teaspoon onion powder
¼ teaspoon caraway seed
Chopped parsley
Crackers

Combine cheese, sour cream, milk, onion powder, and caraway seed; blend well. Refrigerate at least ½ hour before serving. Sprinkle with parsley and serve with crackers. Yield: ⅔ cup.

SHARP GOUDA SPREAD

1 (8-ounce) round Gouda cheese
½ cup finely chopped smoked sliced beef
¼ cup commercial sour cream
2 tablespoons pickle relish
2 teaspoons prepared horseradish

Allow cheese to come to room temperature. Using cookie cutter, cut wax from top of cheese. Carefully remove cheese from shell; keep shell intact. In a small mixing bowl beat cheese until smooth; add beef, sour cream, pickle relish, and horseradish. Refill shell. Yield: 1½ cups.

Creamy Cheese Spread (page 124)

MUSHROOM-CHIVE CHEESE SPREAD

¼ cup canned mushrooms,
chopped

⅓ cup chive-flavored cream
cheese, softened

Combine mushrooms and cream cheese until smooth. Yield: about ½ cup.

PECAN-CHEDDAR SANDWICH SPREAD

4 cups shredded extra sharp
natural Cheddar cheese
½ cup mayonnaise

2 teaspoons prepared mustard
1 cup finely chopped pecans

Combine cheese, mayonnaise, mustard, and pecans; mix well. Store in refrigerator. This is a tangy spread for sandwiches or for snacks. Yield: about 4 cups.

CHEESY PIMIENTO SPREAD

1 (5-ounce) jar pasteurized
Neufchâtel cheese spread
with pimiento
1 (2-ounce) jar chopped
pimiento, drained and finely
chopped

12 pimiento-stuffed olives,
finely chopped
⅓ cup commercial sour cream
½ cup finely chopped pecans
(optional)

Combine all ingredients, and mix well. Yield: about 1½ cups.

Photograph for this recipe on page 111

QUICK-AS-A-WINK CHEESE SPREAD

1 (8-ounce) jar process
cheese spread
¼ teaspoon Worcestershire
sauce

1 teaspoon prepared mustard
2 tablespoons chili sauce
3 dozen crackers or toast
rounds

Combine cheese spread, Worcestershire sauce, mustard, and chili sauce; blend until smooth. Spread about ½ tablespoon of the mixture on each cracker. Yield: 3 dozen.

VALLEY CHEESE SPREAD

2 (3-ounce) packages cream
cheese
4 ounces blue cheese
1 (5-ounce) jar garlic-flavored
cheese spread
¼ cup port

½ cup chopped walnuts
¼ cup chopped parsley
2 tablespoons grated onion
½ teaspoon Worcestershire
sauce

Have cheeses at room temperature. Blend the three cheeses; add remaining ingredients and mix well. Yield: 2 cups.

WALNUT-SMOKED CHEESE SPREAD

¼ cup chopped walnuts
¼ cup smoked cheese spread
½ teaspoon Worcestershire
    sauce

¼ cup mayonnaise

Combine all ingredients and mix well. Yield: ⅔ cup.

WHEAT GERM CHEESE SPREAD

2 cups shredded sharp
    Cheddar cheese
½ cup chopped apples
½ cup chopped walnuts
½ cup chopped celery
½ cup shredded carrots
⅓ cup mayonnaise
2 tablespoons chopped raisins

2 tablespoons chopped dates
2 tablespoons chopped green
    pepper
1 tablespoon wheat germ
1 teaspoon lemon juice
1 teaspoon Worcestershire
    sauce

Combine all ingredients, mixing well. Serve with whole wheat bread or crackers. Yield: 4 cups.

CHOPPED CHICKEN LIVERS

3 tablespoons butter or
    margarine, divided
1 whole clove garlic
2 onions, finely minced
1 pound chicken livers
Salt and pepper

2 hard-cooked eggs
¼ cup melted butter or
    margarine (or half cream
    and half butter)
1 tablespoon sherry (optional)

Heat 2 tablespoons butter and garlic, with a wooden pick in it, in skillet. Add onions and sauté until tender and yellow; do not brown. Discard garlic; turn onions into a bowl. Add a bit more butter to skillet and sauté livers until done: do not overcook. Stir in seasonings; put mixture and eggs through the finest blade of meat grinder. Blend in melted butter and sherry (if desired), stirring until smooth. May be made a day ahead. Leftovers freeze well. Yield: 12 servings.

127

CHICKEN LIVER SANDWICH SPREAD

8 chicken livers (about ¼
  pound)
2 tablespoons salad oil
1 very small onion, finely
  chopped
1 hard-cooked egg, finely
  chopped

¼ teaspoon coarsely ground
  pepper
¼ teaspoon salt
3 tablespoons mayonnaise
Pinch of tarragon (optional)
Chopped parsley (optional)

Dry livers with paper towels. Heat oil in a small frying pan and sauté livers about 5 minutes on each side. Drain livers on paper towel and cool; then finely chop.

    Mix chopped liver with remaining ingredients. Chill. Serve in sandwiches or on buttered toast or crackers. Yield: about 1 cup.

CHICKEN AND MUSHROOM SANDWICH SPREAD

1 cup chopped cooked
  chicken
⅓ cup toasted almonds
  (optional)
1 tablespoon minced onion
1 (3-ounce) can broiled
  mushrooms, chopped

½ cup diced celery
½ teaspoon salt
⅛ teaspoon pepper
½ teaspoon curry powder
½ cup mayonnaise

Put chopped chicken (preferably white meat) through food chopper, using fine cutter. Measure 1 cup and set aside. Put almonds (if desired) through food chopper. Combine chicken with other ingredients; mix well. Yield: 1½ to 2 cups.

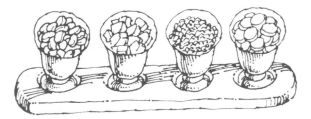

CLAM TEMPTER

1 cup cottage cheese
½ cup canned minced clams,
  chopped
1 tablespoon clam broth
1 clove garlic, finely minced
1 teaspoon lemon juice

1 teaspoon Worcestershire
  sauce
½ teaspoon salt
¼ teaspoon aromatic bitters
Chopped chives (optional)

Mash cottage cheese with a fork until smooth. Combine all ingredients except chives. Spoon into serving bowl. Garnish with chopped chives, if desired. Chill well before serving. Yield: 1½ cups.

CLAM AND CHUTNEY SPREAD

1 (8-ounce) can clams, drained	Dash of Worcestershire sauce
2 (8-ounce) packages cream cheese, softened	Peach or apricot chutney
	Imitation bacon bits
2 tablespoons chopped onion	1 cup chopped chives
	Sesame toast rounds

Combine clams, cream cheese, onion, and Worcestershire sauce in food processor; process with the steel blade until smooth. Pack into a 3-cup mold; chill until serving time. Unmold; spread top with chutney, and sprinkle with bacon bits and chives. Serve with sesame toast rounds. Yield: about 3 cups.

CORNED BEEF SANDWICH SPREAD

1 cup coarsely ground or chopped canned corned beef	½ cup finely chopped celery
	1 teaspoon grated onion
2 teaspoons prepared mustard	Mayonnaise

Combine all ingredients, adding just enough mayonnaise to moisten. Yield: 1½ cups.

NIPPY CORNED BEEF 'N CHEESE BALL

1 (12-ounce) can corned beef, minced	2 teaspoons prepared horseradish
1 (8-ounce) package cream cheese, softened	1½ teaspoons prepared mustard
2 cups shredded Cheddar cheese	½ teaspoon Worcestershire sauce
¾ cup sweet pickle relish	½ teaspoon grated lemon rind
3 tablespoons lemon juice	Snipped fresh parsley

Combine all ingredients except parsley in a large mixing bowl; beat at medium speed of electric mixer until well blended. Chill well, and shape into a ball.

Wrap securely in aluminum foil; chill until 30 minutes before serving. Coat well with parsley. Serve with assorted crackers or as a sandwich spread. Yield: about 3 cups.

EGG APPETIZERS

6 large hard-cooked eggs
½ cup finely chopped ripe
    olives
½ cup butter or margarine,
    softened
2 tablespoons prepared
    mustard

¼ teaspoon salt
¼ teaspoon onion powder
¼ teaspoon hot pepper sauce
Round buttery crackers

Press hard-cooked eggs through a sieve or food mill. Add olives, butter, mustard, salt, onion powder, and hot pepper sauce. Mix well; cover and place in the refrigerator for about 2 hours to allow the flavors to blend. Spread on crackers to serve. Yield about 3 cups.

CHEESE AND EGG APPETIZER

2 (3-ounce) packages cream
    cheese, softened
4 hard-cooked eggs, grated
¼ teaspoon garlic powder
½ teaspoon salt
2 tablespoons dry white Rhine
    wine

⅛ teaspoon hot pepper sauce
½ teaspoon vinegar
Yellow food coloring
Bacon bits
Assorted crackers

Combine first 7 ingredients and blend well. Divide mixture. Add food coloring to ⅓ of the mixture so it resembles an egg yolk. Shape "yolk" and remaining ⅔ of the cheese and egg mixture around it into the shape of an egg. Roll in bacon bits. Chill and serve with assorted crackers. Yield: 2 cups.

FROSTED EGG MOUND

11 hard-cooked eggs
½ cup melted butter or
    margarine
½ teaspoon minced green
    onion
½ to ¾ teaspoon salt

⅛ teaspoon pepper
⅛ teaspoon curry powder
⅓ cup commercial sour cream
Chopped chives
Parsley
Crackers

Line a small round mixing bowl with a large piece of plastic wrap; set aside. Finely chop 8 eggs; add butter, onion, salt, pepper, and curry powder. Mix well, and spoon into mixing bowl; cover and chill at least 3 hours.

Unmold egg mixture onto a serving dish, and spread evenly with sour cream; sprinkle with chives.

Cut remaining 3 eggs in half, and place around mound; garnish with parsley. Serve with crackers. Yield: 3 cups.

Photograph for this recipe on page 9

EGG-PEANUT SPREAD

6 hard-cooked eggs, finely
  chopped
½ cup finely chopped roasted
  peanuts
2 tablespoons finely chopped
  pimiento
2 tablespoons finely chopped
  olives
1 tablespoon finely chopped
  chives
¾ teaspoon salt
¼ cup mayonnaise
¼ cup milk
¼ teaspoon Worcestershire
  sauce
Crackers and potato chips

Combine all finely chopped ingredients and salt. Combine mayonnaise, milk, and Worcestershire sauce; blend with eggs and other ingredients. Stir well. Serve with crackers and potato chips. Yield: 2 cups.

GUACAMOLE MOUSSE

1 envelope unflavored gelatin
1 cup cold water
1 chicken bouillon cube,
  crumbled
¼ teaspoon salt
1½ cups sieved avocado
½ cup commercial sour cream
3 tablespoons finely chopped
  green onion
2 tablespoons lemon juice
½ teaspoon hot sauce
Crackers

Soften gelatin in cold water in a small saucepan. Add bouillon cube and salt. Heat, stirring constantly, until gelatin and bouillon are dissolved; cool slightly.

Combine avocado, sour cream, green onion, lemon juice, and hot sauce; stir in gelatin mixture. Pour into a 3-cup mold and refrigerate until firm. Unmold, and garnish as desired. Serve with crackers. Yield: about 2⅔ cups.

APPETIZER HAM BALL

2 (4½-ounce) cans deviled
  ham
3 tablespoons chopped stuffed
  olives
1 tablespoon prepared mustard
Hot pepper sauce to taste
1 (3-ounce) package cream
  cheese, softened and
  divided
2 teaspoons milk

Combine deviled ham, olives, mustard, hot pepper sauce, and ⅓ of the cream cheese; blend until smooth. Chill. Shape mixture into a ball. Combine remaining cream cheese and milk; frost ham ball with this mixture. Chill. Remove from refrigerator 15 minutes before serving. Yield: 1½ cups.

FROSTED HAM BALL

1 pound cooked ham, ground
½ cup dark seedless raisins
1 medium onion, grated
¾ cup mayonnaise
½ teaspoon curry powder

2 (3-ounce) packages cream
    cheese, softened
2 tablespoons milk
Chopped parsley
Assorted crackers

Combine ham, raisins, onion, mayonnaise, and curry powder. Mold mixture into a round shape on a serving plate. Chill. Blend cream cheese and milk. Frost ham mixture with cream cheese mixture. Garnish with parsley. Serve with assorted crackers. Yield: about 4½ cups.

HAM-AND-EGG SPREAD

3 cups ground cooked ham
¼ cup chopped pickle
1½ teaspoons finely chopped
    pimiento

4 hard-cooked eggs, minced
½ cup mayonnaise

Combine all ingredients, mixing well; chill. Yield: about 3½ cups.

SPICY HAM 'N RAISIN FILLING

1 (4½-ounce) can deviled
    ham
½ cup chopped celery
¼ cup chopped nuts

2 tablespoons mayonnaise
¼ cup chopped seedless
    raisins

Combine all ingredients and mix well. Yield: 1½ cups.

PINTO-DEVILED HAM SPREAD

1 (3-ounce) can deviled ham
1 (3-ounce) package pimiento
    cream cheese, softened

¼ cup diced celery

Combine all ingredients and mix well. Yield: 1 cup.

HOLIDAY HORS D'OEUVRES

1 (3-ounce) package cream
    cheese, softened
1 (4½-ounce) can deviled
    ham

3 tablespoons crushed
    pineapple
Chopped chives
Assorted crackers

Combine first 3 ingredients. Chill. Turn mixture onto a plate; form into a large ball and cover generously with chives. Chill. Serve with assorted crackers. Yield: about 1 cup.

LIVERWURST SALAD SANDWICH SPREAD

1 (4¾-ounce) can liverwurst
    spread
½ cup chopped radish
⅓ cup chopped carrot

1 hard-cooked egg, chopped
1 tablespoon minced onion
Bread

Combine all ingredients except bread. Chill, if desired. Use as a sandwich spread on thin-sliced white, light rye, or party-size bread. Yield: about 1⅓ cups.

OLIVE AND DRIED BEEF SPREAD

1 cup medium white sauce
1 cup shredded sharp Cheddar
    cheese
¼ teaspoon dry mustard
½ teaspoon Worcestershire
    sauce

½ cup sliced ripe olives
¼ cup finely shredded dried
    chipped beef
Corn chips

Put white sauce in top of a double boiler over warm water; gradually add cheese, stirring until melted. Add seasonings and mix well. Stir in olives and dried beef. Transfer to a chafing dish and serve with corn chips. Yield: about 2½ cups.

OLIVE-CHEDDAR SANDWICH SPREAD

4 cups shredded mild Cheddar
    cheese
¾ cup mayonnaise or salad
    dressing
1 (8-ounce) jar
    pimiento-stuffed olives,
    drained and chopped

Bread or toast
Lettuce

Combine cheese, mayonnaise, and olives; stir until well blended. Spread cheese mixture on bread or toast slices. Top with lettuce and additional slices of bread to make sandwiches. Yield: about 4 cups.

CREAMY ORANGE-PECAN FILLING

2 (3-ounce) packages cream
    cheese, softened
2 tablespoons grated orange
    rind

¼ cup orange juice
1 cup chopped pecans

Combine all ingredients and mix well. Yield: about 1¼ cups.

Oyster Spread (below); Bacon-and-Rye Balls (page 61); Snappy Cheese Wafers (page 65)

OYSTER SPREAD

2 (8-ounce) packages cream
  cheese, softened
¼ cup milk or evaporated
  milk
2 to 3 tablespoons
  mayonnaise
1 tablespoon lemon juice
1 tablespoon Worcestershire
  sauce

Dash of hot sauce
Salt to taste
2 (3⅔-ounce) cans smoked
  oysters, minced
Paprika
Chopped parsley

Combine all ingredients except oysters, paprika, and parsley; blend well.
Stir in oysters, and refrigerate several hours. Sprinkle with paprika and
parsley before serving. Yield: about 3 cups.

BELGIAN PÂTÉ

1 (8-ounce) roll
 braunschweiger, softened
1 (8-ounce) package cream
 cheese, softened
¼ cup finely chopped onion
6 slices bacon, cooked and
 crumbled

2 tablespoons minced parsley
2 teaspoons Worcestershire
 sauce
Party rye bread

Combine braunschweiger and cream cheese until well blended; add remaining ingredients except bread, mixing well. Serve on party rye bread. Yield: about 2 cups.

Note: Pâté improves if refrigerated at least 1 day before serving.

CHICKEN LIVER PÂTÉ

1 pound chicken livers
4 hard-cooked eggs
2 medium onions, grated
2 teaspoons salt
¼ teaspoon pepper

2 tablespoons lemon juice
½ cup melted butter or
 margarine
Crackers

Cook chicken livers for 5 minutes in a small amount of boiling water. Drain. Combine with hard-cooked eggs, grated onion, salt, pepper, and lemon juice. Finely chop or put in a blender and mix until smooth. Add melted butter and mix well. Chill at least 2 to 3 hours. Serve with crackers. Yield: about 3 cups.

Photograph for this recipe on page 82

SHERRIED CHICKEN LIVER PÂTÉ

1 pound chicken livers
All-purpose flour seasoned with
 salt and pepper
2 tablespoons butter or
 margarine
1 medium onion, finely
 chopped
¼ cup dry sherry, divided
Pinch of rosemary

Pinch of thyme
6 tablespoons butter or
 margarine, softened
2 tablespoons Cognac
Salt, pepper, and seasoned
 salt to taste
Parsley sprigs
Melba rounds

Pat livers dry with paper towels. Sprinkle lightly with seasoned flour. Heat butter in a skillet and sauté livers over medium heat for about 5 minutes. Add onion and continue cooking and stirring until onion is barely yellow, about 3 minutes. Stir in 2 tablespoons sherry, rosemary, and thyme and simmer for a minute. Add softened butter; remove from heat and puree in electric blender, blending ⅓ of the mixture at a time and pushing down from sides into path of blades. When all has been blended until smooth, stir in remaining 2 tablespoons sherry, Cognac, salt, pepper, and seasoned salt. Chill in container from which pâté is to be served. Garnish with clusters of fresh parsley and serve with melba rounds. Yield: about 2½ cups.

VELVET CHICKEN LIVER PÂTÉ

½ pound chicken livers
2 tablespoons melted butter
⅓ to ½ cup chicken broth
2 hard-cooked eggs, chopped
Salt, pepper, and seasoned
    salt to taste

2 (3-ounce) packages cream
    cheese, softened
2 tablespoons dry sherry
Stuffed olives
Parsley sprigs

Sauté livers in butter about 10 minutes or until just tender. Stir in broth, and swirl in pan a minute; then put in container of electric blender. Add eggs, and blend until smooth.

Combine seasonings and cream cheese; add to liver mixture along with sherry, blending well. Put pâté in an oiled mold or bowl. Chill. Unmold and garnish with olives and parsley. Yield: about 2½ cups.

CONSOMMÉ PÂTÉ MOLD

1 envelope unflavored gelatin
1 pint canned beef consommé,
    divided
2 (3-ounce) packages cream
    cheese, softened
2 tablespoons half-and-half
⅛ teaspoon garlic powder

⅛ teaspoon Beau Monde
    seasoning
Sliced green olives
Pimiento strips
½ cup mashed, fried chicken
    livers

Dissolve gelatin in ¼ cup consommé. Heat the remaining consommé to boiling and add dissolved gelatin. Blend cream cheese and half-and-half; add garlic powder and Beau Monde seasoning. Arrange sliced green olives and pimiento strips in bottom of round mold, and spoon ⅛ cup of the consommé mixture carefully into mold. Place in refrigerator until set; then add the remainder and return to refrigerator. Add mashed livers to cream cheese mixture and spread over congealed consommé (may be made the day before). Yield: about 3 cups.

PARTY TIME PÂTÉ

2 (4¾-ounce) cans liverwurst
    spread
½ cup butter or margarine,
    softened
2 tablespoons minced onion
¾ teaspoon salt

¼ teaspoon ground nutmeg
1 teaspoon dry mustard
⅛ teaspoon ground cloves
Dash of cayenne pepper
Rye crackers

Combine all ingredients except crackers. Cover tightly and chill for at least 4 hours. Serve with rye crackers. Yield: about 1½ cups.

DEVILED PEANUT SPREAD

½ cup peanut butter (smooth or crunchy)
1 (2¼-ounce) can deviled ham

½ teaspoon celery salt
Crackers

Combine first 3 ingredients. Serve on crackers. Yield: ¾ cup.

PEANUT BUTTER-BACON SPREAD

4 slices bacon
½ cup peanut butter (smooth or crunchy)
½ cup finely chopped dill pickle

2 tablespoons dill pickle juice
¼ teaspoon salt
Dash of hot pepper sauce
Crackers

Cook bacon until crisp. Drain on paper towels. Crumble into small pieces. Mix with peanut butter, dill pickle, juice, and seasonings. Serve on crackers. Yield: about 1 cup.

BUTTERED PIMIENTO SPREAD

½ cup butter or margarine, softened
¼ pound pimiento cream cheese, softened
1 tablespoon grated onion
½ teaspoon Worcestershire sauce
1 teaspoon lemon juice

1 tablespoon minced green pepper
1 teaspoon caraway seed
1 (2-ounce) can anchovies, drained
Several grinds coarse black pepper
Melba rounds

Cream butter and cheese together in large bowl of electric mixer. Add remaining ingredients except melba rounds, and blend well. Chill and serve with melba rounds. Yield: about 1 cup.

Note: If pimiento cream cheese is not available, use ¼ pound cream cheese into which a small jar of drained pimiento strips has been blended.

PINEAPPLE SANDWICH MIXTURE

15 large marshmallows
Juice of 1 lemon
1 (8¼-ounce) can crushed pineapple

1 (8-ounce) package dates, chopped
1 cup chopped nuts
1 cup mayonnaise

Combine marshmallows, lemon juice, and pineapple in a double boiler or heavy pan; heat until marshmallows are melted. Let cool; add dates and nuts. Stir in mayonnaise. Yield: about 2 cups.

RAISIN SANDWICH SPREAD

1 egg
1 cup sugar
Juice and rind of 1½ lemons
1 teaspoon butter or margarine

1 cup ground seedless raisins
1 cup mayonnaise
Thinly sliced whole wheat
    bread

Beat egg until light colored. Combine egg, sugar, lemon juice and rind, and butter in a medium saucepan. Cook over low heat, stirring constantly, until thickened. Cool. Stir in raisins and mayonnaise. Cool thoroughly. Spread on whole wheat bread. Yield: about 2½ cups.

Photograph for this recipe on page 154

RUMAKI SPREAD

½ pound chicken livers
Salt and pepper
Butter or margarine
1 tablespoon soy sauce
½ cup butter or margarine,
    softened
½ teaspoon onion salt
½ teaspoon dry mustard
¼ teaspoon ground nutmeg
1 or 2 dashes of cayenne
    pepper

1 (5-ounce) can water
    chestnuts, drained and
    minced
6 slices crisp cooked bacon,
    crumbled
Thinly sliced green onions for
    garnish (optional)
Crackers

Cook chicken livers seasoned with salt and pepper in butter. When done, place in blender with soy sauce, ½ cup butter, onion salt, mustard, nutmeg, and cayenne pepper. Blend until mixture is smooth, stirring it down with rubber spatula as needed. Remove from blender; stir in chestnuts and bacon; garnish with onions, if desired. Serve with crisp crackers. Yield: 1½ cups.

Note: This spread should be prepared a day ahead of serving but should be removed from refrigerator and allowed to soften slightly at room temperature for 1 hour before serving.

SALMON BALL

1 (7¾-ounce) can red salmon,
    drained and flaked
1 (8-ounce) package cream
    cheese, softened
1 tablespoon lemon juice
2 teaspoons grated onion

1 teaspoon prepared
    horseradish
¼ teaspoon salt
¼ teaspoon liquid smoke
Chopped parsley

Combine all ingredients except parsley. Shape into a ball; roll ball in parsley. Yield: 1 cheese ball.

SHRIMP SPREAD

1 (4½-ounce) can shrimp, drained
1 (3-ounce) package cream cheese, softened
1 small onion, grated

¼ teaspoon Worcestershire sauce
2 teaspoons mustard-flavored sandwich and salad sauce
Garlic powder to taste

Mash shrimp with a fork; add remaining ingredients, beating well. Chill mixture for several hours to blend flavors. Yield: about 1 cup.

Photograph for this recipe on page 111

SHRIMP MOUSSE

1 (10¾-ounce) can tomato soup, undiluted
1 (8-ounce) package cream cheese, softened
1½ envelopes unflavored gelatin
¼ cup cold water

1 cup mayonnaise
2 (4½-ounce) cans shrimp
1 tablespoon Worcestershire sauce
3 stalks celery
6 scallions or 1 medium onion
Salt and pepper to taste

Warm soup and cheese in a saucepan over low heat until cheese melts. Soften gelatin in cold water; add to soup and stir over heat until gelatin dissolves. Put cheese mixture and remaining ingredients in a blender and blend until smooth. Pour into a 1-quart mold and refrigerate overnight. Unmold and garnish as desired. Yield: 4 cups.

Note: Mousse may be made several days before serving. Garnish with black caviar, grated egg yolk, parsley sprigs, and pimiento strips. Serve as a spread on crackers or bread.

Photograph for this recipe on cover

TUNA SOUR CREAM FILLING

1 (7-ounce) can tuna, drained and flaked
¼ cup chopped celery
2 tablespoons minced onion

2 tablespoons pickle relish
6 tablespoons commercial sour cream

Combine ingredients and mix well. Use as a sandwich filling or a spread for crackers. Yield: 1¼ cups.

FRESH VEGETABLE SPREAD

1 small onion
1 small carrot
½ cucumber
1 (8-ounce) package cream cheese, softened

1 to 2 tablespoons mayonnaise

Grate onion, carrot, and cucumber; drain well. Add vegetables to cream cheese and mayonnaise; beat well. Chill several hours to blend flavors. Yield: about 1½ cups.

Photograph for this recipe on page 111

Tangy-Sweet Meatballs (page 37); Smoked Egg Dip (page 98);
Open-Faced Mini-Reubens (page 152)

canapés

Canapés consist of bite-size pieces of bread, crackers, or pastry topped with a spread or pieces of meat, cheese, or vegetables. Canapés can be either hot or cold, but are always open-faced.

When using bread as the base for canapés the crust is always removed. It's easier to trim crust off fresh bread if the bread is frozen.

Spread slices of bread with softened butter or margarine before spreading with filling; this prevents filling from soaking into the bread and making it soggy. Be sure to spread filling all the way to the edges of bread; that way, there are no dry edges.

Some canapés can be prepared one to two weeks ahead and frozen, depending on the filling. Most meat, cream cheese, and sour cream fillings freeze well; do not freeze fillings that contain cooked egg white, fresh vegetables, and jellies. Mayonnaise and salad dressing separate when frozen, so avoid freezing fillings that contain them.

141

ANCHOVY ROLL-UPS

1 (3-ounce) package cream
  cheese, softened
1 tablespoon milk
1½ to 2 teaspoons anchovy
  paste

1 teaspoon Worcestershire
  sauce
Bread
3 tablespoons melted butter or
  margarine

Blend cream cheese and milk until creamy (add more milk if necessary).
Blend in anchovy paste and Worcestershire sauce. Trim crusts from bread.
Spread on mixture and roll up. Wrap in waxed paper and store in
refrigerator until ready to serve. The rolls may also be frozen. To serve,
sauté rolls in melted butter. Rolls may be cut in half, if desired. Stick
wooden picks in them and serve hot. Yield: 10 servings.

AVOCADO FINGERS

1 ripe avocado
¼ teaspoon salt
⅛ teaspoon paprika

1 teaspoon lemon juice
Toast strips
Bacon slices

Mash avocado; add salt, paprika, and lemon juice. Spread on 3- x 1-inch
toast strips. Place narrow slices of bacon over avocado. Broil until bacon
crisps. Yield: about 24 servings.

AVOCADO-CHEESE FOLDOVERS

1 cup mashed avocado pulp
¼ cup Roquefort cheese
1 tablespoon lemon juice

Thinly sliced white bread
Softened butter or margarine

Combine avocado, cheese, and lemon juice. Remove crusts from bread;
roll lightly with a rolling pin. Spread butter on bread. Cut each slice into
quarters. Place about 1 teaspoonful of the avocado mixture on each
square. Fold two opposite corners over and secure with a wooden pick.
Cover and chill for 15 minutes. Remove wooden pick before serving.
Yield: about 4 dozen.

BACON-CHEESE FINGERS

1 cup shredded Swiss cheese
8 slices bacon, cooked and
  crumbled
3 to 4 tablespoons
  mayonnaise

1 tablespoon grated onion
½ teaspoon celery salt
10 slices day-old sandwich
  bread, crusts removed and
  cut into thirds

Combine first 5 ingredients; blend well. Spread cheese mixture over each
piece of bread. Bake at 325° for 10 minutes. Yield: 30 appetizers.

CANAPÉS

1 (8-ounce) package cream
  cheese, softened
1 egg yolk

1 teaspoon grated onion
¼ teaspoon Ac'cent
Crackers

Combine all ingredients except crackers and mix well. Spread on crackers and broil. The canapés puff up and turn golden brown. Yield: 2 dozen.

CANAPÉ MAYONNAISE

1 envelope unflavored gelatin
¼ cup cold water

1 cup mayonnaise

Soften gelatin in cold water. Place over hot water and stir until gelatin is completely dissolved. Add to mayonnaise and blend well. Mayonnaise glaze may be stored in a tightly covered container in refrigerator. It will "moistureproof" your crisp crackers or bread and form a canapé base. Yield: 1¼ cups.

BROILED CHEESE APPETIZERS

2 (3-ounce) packages cream
  cheese, softened
1 cup shredded provolone
  cheese
1 tablespoon chopped onion
½ teaspoon oregano

⅛ teaspoon garlic salt
1 tablespoon chopped
  pimiento
1 tablespoon chopped green
  pepper
Toast rounds

Beat cream cheese until smooth; add provolone cheese, onion, oregano, and garlic salt. Stir in pimiento and green pepper. Spread on toast; broil for 1 to 2 minutes or until lightly browned. Serve immediately. Yield: 1½ cups spread.

CHEESE-HAM CANAPÉS

1 cup shredded Cheddar
  cheese
½ cup finely chopped cooked
  ham
¼ cup pickle relish

¼ cup commercial sour cream
1 (1-pound) loaf unsliced
  sandwich bread
Butter or margarine, softened
Sliced cooked ham

Combine cheese, ham, relish, and sour cream. Cut crusts from bread. Slice lengthwise into 3 or 4 strips. Butter each strip, then spread with cheese mixture. When ready to serve, place on a cookie sheet, and broil 3 inches from source of heat until cheese melts. Top with triangles or diamonds of cooked ham. Cut into 1-inch strips for serving. Yield: about 3 to 4 dozen.

CURRIED CHEESE APPETIZERS

1½ cups shredded sharp
  Cheddar cheese
½ cup mayonnaise
½ cup finely chopped green
  onion
½ cup finely chopped ripe
  olives

½ teaspoon curry powder
1 (6½-ounce) package whole
  wheat wafers
Additional ripe olives, sliced

Combine first 5 ingredients; stir until well blended. Spread about 1 teaspoon mixture on each wafer; broil until cheese melts. Garnish with olive slices, and serve hot. Yield: about 5 dozen.

Nutty Stuffed Celery (page 63); Curried Cheese Appetizers (above)

CHEESE DREAMS

½ cup milk	Rounds of white bread
1 egg, beaten	Melted butter or margarine
¼ teaspoon dry mustard	Paprika
½ teaspoon salt	
3 cups shredded sharp	
Cheddar cheese	

Heat milk in top of a double boiler over hot water. When milk is scalded, add egg, mustard, salt, and cheese; cook for 15 minutes, stirring constantly. Remove from heat; cool, cover, and store in refrigerator.

When ready to use, spread cheese mixture on rounds of white bread, cover with another round in which you have cut a small hole in middle with inside of doughnut cutter. Brush with melted butter, sprinkle with paprika, and bake at 450° until nicely browned. Serve immediately. Yield: 15 servings.

TOASTED CHEESE ROUNDS

⅓ cup grated Parmesan	Dash of Worcestershire sauce
cheese	Dash of salt
¾ cup mayonnaise	Dash of pepper
½ cup chopped onion	Rye bread rounds

Combine all ingredients except bread; mix well. Spread mixture on bread; broil until golden brown. Yield: 20 rounds.

TOASTED GARLIC-CHEESE ROUNDS

½ cup butter or margarine	About 1 cup grated Parmesan
2 cloves garlic, slashed	and shredded Swiss
1 day-old loaf sliced white	cheese, mixed (or mixed
bread	Parmesan and Gruyère)

Combine butter and garlic in a small saucepan and heat until butter bubbles. Remove from heat, let stand for about 3 hours, then discard the garlic.

Cut crusts from bread and with a cookie cutter cut into circles about 1½ to 2 inches in diameter. Arrange on cookie sheets, brush with garlic butter, and sprinkle generously with cheese. Bake at 275° to 300° until crisp. Yield: about 3 dozen.

HOT CHEESE SQUARES

1 loaf white bread, unsliced
½ cup butter or margarine
1 (3-ounce) package cream
    cheese, softened

¼ cup shredded sharp cheese
2 egg whites

Trim crusts from bread; cut into 1-inch slices, then cut each slice into quarters. Melt butter; blend in cheeses. Beat egg whites until stiff; fold into cooled cheese mixture. Spread cheese mixture on all sides of bread cubes; refrigerate at least overnight. If preferred, squares may be frozen at this point. Bake at 400° for about 15 minutes or until nicely browned; serve hot. Yield: about 5 dozen.

CHICKEN TEMPTERS

8 slices soft white bread
Softened butter or margarine
1 (4¾-ounce) can chicken
    spread

¼ cup minced celery
½ to ¾ teaspoon basil
Pimiento strips

Remove crusts from bread and flatten bread with rolling pin. Lightly butter both sides of bread. Bring two diagonally opposite corners of each piece of bread together and secure with a wooden pick. Bake on an ungreased cookie sheet at 400° for 7 to 8 minutes. Remove picks and cool on a wire rack about 30 minutes. Combine chicken spread, celery, and basil; fill bread. Garnish with pimiento strips. Yield: 8 sandwiches.

BROILED CLAM CANAPÉS

1 (3-ounce) package chive
    cream cheese, softened
½ teaspoon salt
1 tablespoon lemon juice
3 drops hot pepper sauce

1 (7-ounce) can minced
    clams, drained
1 egg white, stiffly beaten
Crackers or toast
Paprika

Combine cheese, salt, lemon juice, pepper sauce, and clams; fold into stiffly beaten egg white. Spread on crackers or toast. Sprinkle with paprika. Broil about 3 inches from source of heat for 2 to 3 minutes or until brown. Serve at once. Yield: 3 dozen.

CRAB CANAPÉS

1 pound crabmeat
3 tablespoons mayonnaise or
    salad dressing
1 tablespoon prepared mustard
¼ teaspoon salt
Dash of pepper

1 tablespoon lemon juice
12 slices white bread
¼ cup grated Parmesan
    cheese
2 tablespoons dry
    breadcrumbs

Remove any shell or cartilage from crabmeat. Combine mayonnaise, seasonings, lemon juice, and crabmeat. Remove crusts and toast bread. Spread crab mixture on each slice of toast. Combine cheese and bread-crumbs; sprinkle over top of each slice of toast. Cut each slice into 6 pieces. Broil about 3 inches from source of heat for 2 to 3 minutes or until brown. Yield: 6 dozen.

HOT CRAB CANAPÉS

¾ to 1 cup crabmeat, flaked	1 teaspoon lemon juice
¼ cup mayonnaise	1 egg white, stiffly beaten
¼ teaspoon salt	Bread squares or salted
Dash of pepper	crackers
4 to 6 drops hot pepper sauce	

Combine crabmeat, mayonnaise, seasonings, and lemon juice. Fold beaten egg white into mixture. Cut crusts from bread and cut each slice into four squares. Spread mixture all over bread. Broil 4 to 5 inches from heat for 2 or 3 minutes. Leftover crab makes a good open-face sandwich the next day. Yield: about 1¼ cups spread.

CHEESY CRAB CANAPÉS

36 bread slices	Dash of pepper
1 cup flaked crabmeat	1 tablespoon minced parsley
¼ cup mayonnaise	1 tablespoon minced chives
1 teaspoon tarragon vinegar	Grated Parmesan cheese
½ teaspoon dry mustard	Paprika
¼ teaspoon salt	

Cut bread in desired shapes; toast one side. Combine crabmeat, mayonnaise, vinegar, seasonings, parsley, and chives. Spread crab mixture on untoasted sides of bread. Sprinkle with cheese and paprika. Place on a cookie sheet and, just before serving, broil 3 inches from source of heat until brown. Yield: 3 dozen.

CRABMEAT-BACON ROUNDS

½ cup shredded sharp Cheddar cheese	20 (2-inch) toast rounds, buttered
1 (6½-ounce) can crabmeat, drained and flaked	3 slices uncooked bacon, diced
2 egg whites, stiffly beaten	Sliced stuffed green olives

Fold shredded cheese and crabmeat into stiffly beaten egg whites. Pile mixture on 20 buttered toast rounds (made by cutting 2-inch circles from loaf bread, browned on both sides and lightly buttered on top). Sprinkle diced bacon on top of each; broil until cheese starts to melt and bacon is crisp. Top each with a slice of stuffed olive. Yield: 20 appetizers.

Note: To freeze ahead of time, prepare for broiler, place on a flat pan wrapped in moisture-vaporproof paper, and freeze. Remove from freezer and broil.

DEVILED HAM NIPS

8 slices white bread	⅓ cup commercial sour cream
Butter or margarine	⅓ cup shredded Cheddar cheese
1 (4½-ounce) can deviled ham	

Remove crusts from bread, butter lightly, and cut each slice into four squares. Press squares buttered side down into very small muffin pans or place squares on a cookie sheet. To each add a dab of deviled ham, sour cream, and a topping of cheese. Bake at 400° for 5 minutes or until hot and bubbly. Yield: 32 canapés.

HAM AND CHEESE CANAPÉS

1 cup shredded Cheddar cheese	¼ cup commercial sour cream
½ cup finely chopped cooked ham	1 (1-pound) loaf unsliced sandwich bread
¼ cup sweet pickle relish	Butter or margarine, softened

Combine cheese, ham, relish, and sour cream. Cut crusts from bread. Slice bread lengthwise into four 3- x 7-inch strips. Place on heavy-duty aluminum foil-lined cookie sheets. Butter each strip, then spread about ⅓ cup cheese mixture on each. Broil 3 inches from source of heat until cheese melts. Cut into 1½- x 1-inch pieces for serving. Yield: 56 canapés.

BROILED OLIVE CANAPÉS

Sliced white bread
2 tablespoons butter or
   margarine, softened
1 cup shredded sharp process
   American cheese

½ cup chopped stuffed olives
2 egg whites, stiffly beaten
3 slices bacon, finely diced
Olive slices

Cut 20 bread rounds with a 2-inch cookie cutter. Place under broiler and toast on one side. Butter untoasted side. Fold cheese and olives into egg whites; spoon on buttered side of bread rounds. Sprinkle with bacon. Top each with an olive slice. Broil 4 to 5 inches from source of heat for 5 to 8 minutes or until bacon browns and cheese melts. Yield: 20 canapés.

OLIVE AND CRABMEAT CANAPÉS

⅓ cup pitted ripe olives, well
   drained, coarsely chopped
1 (7¾-ounce) can crabmeat,
   drained and flaked
1 tablespoon minced green
   pepper

¼ teaspoon grated lemon rind
Mayonnaise
Firm white bread
Softened butter or margarine
Minced parsley

Combine olives, crabmeat, green pepper, and lemon rind. Mix with just enough mayonnaise so mixture holds together. Cut bread into rounds with a large cookie cutter; butter and bake at 300° until lightly browned. Spread with the crab mixture and sprinkle with parsley. Yield: about 1½ dozen.

TOASTED ONION CANAPÉS

20 (2-inch) bread rounds
¾ cup minced onion
½ cup mayonnaise or salad
   dressing

¼ cup grated Parmesan
   cheese

Place bread rounds on a cookie sheet and toast one side under broiler just until golden brown. Combine onion, mayonnaise, and cheese; spread on untoasted side of bread rounds. Broil 3 inches from source of heat for 2 to 3 minutes or until golden brown. Yield: 20 canapés.

TOASTED ONION STICKS

1 (1⅜-ounce) package dry onion soup mix
½ pound butter or margarine, softened

1 loaf sliced white bread

Blend onion soup mix into butter. Let stand at room temperature until you are ready to toast the sticks.

Trim crusts from bread. Spread with onion butter; cut each slice into three strips. Place on an ungreased cookie sheet and bake at 350° for about 10 minutes or until golden. Yield: about 4½ dozen.

HOT ONION-CHEESE CANAPÉS

8 slices bread or 32 salted crackers
½ cup mayonnaise
½ cup grated Parmesan cheese

2 tablespoons finely chopped onion

Remove crusts from bread; cut each slice into quarters. Combine mayonnaise, cheese, and onion. Spread on bread. Broil about 4 inches from source of heat until brown. Yield: 32 canapés.

Note: Mixture keeps several days in refrigerator.

ONION WITH PEANUT BUTTER

1 cup peanut butter
1 large onion, finely grated
⅛ teaspoon salt

Butter or margarine
Small rolls

Combine peanut butter, onion, and salt. Split and butter small rolls; spread with peanut butter mixture and toast under broiler until delicately browned. Yield: 1½ to 2 dozen.

OYSTER CANAPÉS

1 cup cracker crumbs
½ cup melted butter or margarine
⅓ cup commercial sour cream
1 egg, slightly beaten
2 tablespoons grated onion

1 tablespoon prepared horseradish
½ teaspoon paprika
12 to 16 toast triangles
12 to 16 oysters

Combine cracker crumbs, butter, sour cream, egg, onion, horseradish, and paprika. Spread on toast triangles. Top each with an oyster. Bake at 400° for 15 minutes. Serve hot. Yield: 12 to 16 canapés.

PEANUT BUTTER-BACON CANAPÉS

6 slices bacon
¾ cup peanut butter
¾ cup pickle relish

2 (8-ounce) cans refrigerated
biscuits

Fry bacon until crisp; drain on absorbent paper and crumble. Mix bacon, peanut butter, and pickle relish; beat until well blended. Press biscuits into 3-inch circles. Spoon 1 tablespoon of the peanut butter filling on each circle. Moisten edges of dough with water. Fold over to enclose filling and press edges together with the tines of a fork. Prick tops. Bake at 400° for 10 to 12 minutes or until lightly browned. Serve warm. Yield: 20 canapés.

PIROSHKI (RUSSIAN)

Pastry:

½ cup drained, small curd
  cottage cheese
½ cup butter or margarine

1½ cups all-purpose flour
½ teaspoon sugar
Filling

Have cottage cheese and butter at room temperature. Blend this mixture with flour and sugar until smooth. Form into a flattish ball, wrap in waxed paper, and store in vegetable crisper (so it won't get too cold) in refrigerator overnight. (With this as a basic dough, you can make a variety of canapés and desserts.)

When ready to use, remove from refrigerator and let stand until dough is workable. For the meat filling, roll basic dough ⅛ inch thick on a floured pastry cloth. Cut into 2½-inch squares or in circles with biscuit cutter. Place teaspoon of Filling on one-half of square or circle and fold other half over until edges meet. (Make a triangle of the square.) Moisten edges; seal by pressing tines of fork firmly into edge. Now stand circle or triangle on long side on cookie sheet with seal up; turn one corner toward you, and the other away from you, so that the pastry will rest on cookie sheet with sealed edges up. Bake at 425° until pastry is golden brown, about 15 to 20 minutes. Piroshki can be served cold with hot soup or as a hot canapé. Yield: 1 dozen.

Filling:

½ pound finely ground beef
½ cup minced onions
Butter or margarine
2 hard-cooked eggs, finely
  chopped
1 teaspoon capers

1 teaspoon chopped chives
1 teaspoon chopped parsley
Salt and pepper to taste
1 teaspoon commercial sour
  cream

Sauté meat and onions in a small amount of butter until meat turns gray. Add chopped eggs, capers, chives, parsley, salt, pepper, and sour cream. Use to fill Pastry. Yield: filling for 12 piroshkis.

OPEN-FACED MINI-REUBENS

½ cup Thousand Island
    dressing
24 slices party rye bread
1½ cups well-drained chopped
    sauerkraut

½ pound thinly sliced corned
    beef
¼ pound sliced Swiss cheese

Spread ½ teaspoon dressing on each slice of bread. Place 1 tablespoon sauerkraut on each slice of bread, and top with a slice of corned beef. Cut cheese the size of bread, and place over corned beef.

Arrange sandwiches on a baking sheet; bake at 400° for 10 minutes or until cheese melts. Yield: 2 dozen.

Photograph for this recipe on page 140

SCALLOP CANAPÉS

2 cloves garlic, finely chopped
2 tablespoons melted butter or
    margarine
½ cup shredded cheese
¼ teaspoon Worcestershire
    sauce

Dash of salt
Dash of pepper
½ pound cooked scallops,
    chopped
2 cups piecrust mix

Sauté garlic in butter for 2 to 3 minutes; add cheese, seasonings, and scallops. Blend well. Prepare piecrust mix according to package directions; roll very thin and cut into 90 circles, 2 inches in diameter. Place about 1 teaspoonful scallop filling in the center of 45 circles. Cover with remaining 45 circles; press edges together with a fork and put slits in tops. Place on lightly greased cookie sheets. Bake at 450° for 10 to 15 minutes or until brown. Yield: about 45 canapés.

SHOWTIME ROLL-UPS

2 cups shredded Cheddar
    cheese
1 (3-ounce) package cream
    cheese, softened
2 tablespoons dry roasted
    peanuts, chopped

½ teaspoon Worcestershire
    sauce
Dash of salt
25 slices white sandwich
    bread

Combine cheeses, peanuts, Worcestershire sauce, and salt; mix well. Remove crusts from bread slices; between sheets of waxed paper, flatten with rolling pin. Spread each slice with a tablespoon of cheese mixture; roll up. Place seam side down on tray; cover with sheet of waxed paper and dampened paper towel until ready to serve. Yield: 25 sandwiches.

▪ *Sprinkle freshly cut avocados, bananas, apples, and peaches with lemon juice to prevent darkening.*

SHRIMP-CHEESE PUFFS

½ cup butter or margarine,
   softened
2 cups shredded Cheddar
   cheese
1 egg yolk

1 egg white, stiffly beaten
30 bread squares
30 shrimp, cooked and
   cleaned

Cream butter and cheese; blend in egg yolk. Fold in stiffly beaten egg white. Arrange bread squares on ungreased cookie sheets. Top each with a shrimp and cover with a rounded teaspoonful of cheese mixture. Bake at 350° for 15 to 18 minutes or until golden brown. This may be refrigerated up to 24 hours before baking. Yield: 2½ dozen.

1 (5-ounce) jar dried beef,
   chopped
1 (8-ounce) carton commercial
   sour cream
¾ cup shredded Swiss cheese

25 slices bread, cut in star
   shapes
Commercial sour cream

Combine beef, sour cream, and cheese; mix well. Cover and refrigerate. Spread bread with beef spread. Serve topped with sour cream. Yield: 25 sandwiches.

SHRIMP TOPPERS WITH LEMON-CHILI SAUCE

1 cup chili sauce
1 teaspoon lemon juice
Dash of hot pepper sauce

24 toast rounds
24 cooked shrimp
Parsley sprigs

Combine chili sauce, lemon juice, and hot pepper sauce; spread on toast rounds. Top each with a cooked shrimp and a sprig of parsley. Yield: 2 dozen.

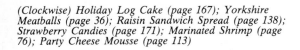

(Clockwise) Holiday Log Cake (page 167); Yorkshire Meatballs (page 36); Raisin Sandwich Spread (page 138); Strawberry Candies (page 171); Marinated Shrimp (page 76); Party Cheese Mousse (page 113)

dainty party fare

Dainty party foods are the perfect food to serve for informal daytime parties, teas, or receptions. For any of these occasions our assortment of dainty sandwiches and hors d'oeuvres is sure to please.

With the sandwich filling recipes included here and the instructions illustrated in the sketches, it's easy to shape tasty sandwiches into pinwheel, ribbon, and checkerboard designs. Other sandwich-making tips are included.

PARTY SANDWICHES

Dainty party sandwiches are the perfect food to serve for informal daytime parties, teas, or receptions. A base of bread or other baked foods, a complementing filling, a pretty garnish, and an unusual cut: this is all that is needed to make intriguing party sandwiches.

Choosing Interesting Breads

Any bread may be used for a sandwich base, but bread and filling should be compatible. Party sandwiches are prettier on thinly sliced bread, and day-old bread holds its shape nicely while being sliced. Crusts are usually removed for dainty sandwiches. It's easier to trim crust off fresh bread if the bread is frozen. For variety, try rye, whole wheat, or cracked wheat bread, or you may bake your own raisin, date-nut, or Boston brown bread. Using two kinds of bread in one sandwich gives added color.

Selecting Complementing Fillings

Filling should be generous, but too much makes the sandwich difficult to handle. Several thin slices of meat rather than one thick slice make a more manageable sandwich. Fillings of pastel colors make eye-appealing sandwiches. Season fillings to accent and complement the flavor of the bread.

Preparing Sandwiches

Prepare all the fillings first and let them stand while you prepare the bread. Bread should be spread with softened butter or margarine so filling does not soak into bread and make it soggy. Spread filling to edge of bread.

Storing Sandwiches

Store sandwiches properly to insure freshness. Line a shallow pan with a damp towel; cover towel with waxed paper. Stack sandwiches in pan, putting waxed paper between each layer. Cover with waxed paper and a damp towel. Most party sandwiches can be made a day in advance and stored in the refrigerator.

Some sandwiches may be made ahead and frozen. Layer them in a suitable container and wrap with moistureproof and vaporproof wrapping and seal. Ribbon, checkerboard, and pinwheel sandwiches can all be wrapped and frozen uncut. They will slice more neatly if cut before thawing. Thaw, in their wrapper, for 1 to 2 hours before serving. Since mayonnaise, salad dressing, and jelly do not freeze well, sandwich fillings may be bound with seasoned butter or seasoned sour cream and then the sandwiches frozen. Avoid freezing sandwiches with fillings containing raw vegetables, dates, pickles, cooked egg whites, olives, or pimientos. Sandwich fillings that do freeze well include peanut butter, cooked egg yolks, and blue cheese.

Shaping Sandwiches

Ribbon

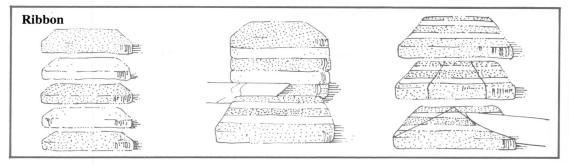

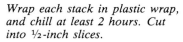

Stack 3 slices whole wheat and 2 slices white bread alternately, filling with 1 or more spreads. Press each stack together firmly, and trim off crusts.

Wrap each stack in plastic wrap, and chill at least 2 hours. Cut into ½-inch slices.

Cut each slice into thirds or halves, and place on serving tray. If not served immediately, cover with waxed paper and a damp towel; store in refrigerator.

Checkerboard

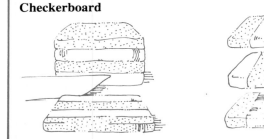

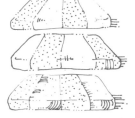

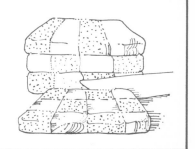

Stack 2 slices whole wheat and 2 slices white bread alternately, filling with 1 or more spreads. Press each stack together, and trim crusts. Cut into ½-inch slices.

Stack 3 slices together so that whole wheat and white strips alternate, filling with 1 or more spreads.

Wrap in plastic wrap, and chill several hours. Remove from refrigerator, and cut into ½-inch checkerboard slices. Cover with waxed paper and damp towel until serving time; store in refrigerator.

Roll-Ups

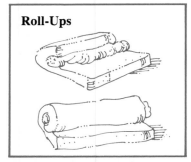

Trim crusts. Spread bread with filling. Lay an asparagus tip or stuffed celery across one end of each slice. Roll up. Roll-ups may be brushed with melted butter and toasted under broiler.

Cornucopias

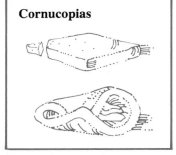

Trim crusts. Cut off ½ inch of bottom corner. Spread bread with filling. Overlap and press opposite corners; garnish.

Envelopes

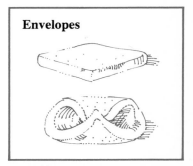

Trim crusts from bread slices. Spread bread with filling. Fold 2 corners together and press firmly.

157

PINWHEEL

Trim crust off a long loaf of unsliced bread. Slice loaf lengthwise into ¼-inch-thick slices, and roll each slice with a rolling pin to flatten. Spread with softened butter and a filling.

If desired, place olives, pickles, Vienna sausage, or a frankfurter across the short end of slice; roll up tightly. Wrap in plastic wrap; and chill several hours or overnight.

Cut chilled rolls into ½-inch slices, and place on serving trays. Cover with waxed paper and a damp towel until ready to serve; store in refrigerator.

CORNUCOPIAS

Remove crusts from bread slices; cut bread into triangles. Spread triangles with mixture of mayonnaise and mustard-with-horseradish. With longest edge of triangle on bottom, place ham strip in center with tip extending over point of triangle. Roll from left to right and tuck point under.

DIAGONAL LOGS

Remove crusts from bread slices. Roll flat with rolling pin. Spread with mixture of mashed avocado, lemon juice, and mayonnaise. Roll bread as for a jelly roll. Cut each log diagonally into two or three parts.

FINGER SANDWICHES

Buy large loaves of unsliced bread from your bakery and cut thin slices, crosswise, with an electric carving knife. Remove crusts; spread with butter and then with filling. Sandwiches may be cut in narrow strips or rolled and cut into finger lengths. Keep covered with a damp tea towel until time to serve.

Ginger-Cream Cheese Filling: Thoroughly mix 1 (8-ounce) package softened cream cheese, 2 tablespoons light rum, and ¼ cup finely minced candied ginger. Yield: enough filling for 25 finger sandwiches.

Chicken-Almond Filling: Grind together 2 cups chopped chicken and ½ cup blanched almonds. Stir in 2 tablespoons drained crushed pineapple and enough mayonnaise to make a spreadable mixture. Yield: filling for 25 to 30 finger sandwiches.

Roquefort-Avocado Filling: Mix together ¼ cup crumbled Roquefort, 1 cup avocado puree, and lemon juice to make a spreadable mixture. Yield: filling for 25 finger sandwiches.

Cheddar-Port Filling: Blend 1 (4-ounce) jar Cheddar cheese spread with 1 to 2 tablespoons port. Yield: filling for 15 finger sandwiches.

ROLLED SANDWICHES

1 (3-ounce) package cream cheese, softened	1 cup chopped watercress
1 teaspoon lemon juice	18 slices white bread
⅓ cup commercial sour cream	2 tablespoons butter or margarine, softened
⅛ teaspoon salt	Watercress sprigs
1 teaspoon chopped chives	

Blend cream cheese, lemon juice, sour cream, salt, and chives. Stir in chopped watercress. Trim crusts from bread and roll slices lightly with a rolling pin to make them more pliable. Spread bread with soft butter, then with watercress mixture. Roll like a jelly roll.

Arrange close together, seam side down, in a shallow pan. Cover with plastic wrap or heavy-duty aluminum foil and chill for at least 1 hour.

To serve, slice each roll-up crosswise into two lengths (each about 1½ inches long). Stand them upright and insert sprigs of watercress in top. Yield: 3 dozen.

ROLLED MUSHROOM SANDWICHES

1 (3-ounce) can mushrooms, drained	¼ teaspoon ground nutmeg
1 tablespoon lemon juice	Salt and pepper to taste
1 (3-ounce) package cream cheese, softened	24 slices thinly sliced fresh bread
1 tablespoon mayonnaise	Small bunch of parsley

Chop mushrooms into bits and add lemon juice. Mix cream cheese, mayonnaise, nutmeg, and salt and pepper. Add mushrooms and mix well.

Remove crusts from bread and spread with mushroom mixture. Roll slices and fasten with wooden pick. Place in a pan lined with a damp cloth and cover with a damp cloth. Chill well. Remove wooden picks before serving. Insert a small spray of parsley in each end of the sandwich. Yield: 2 dozen.

SESAME-CHEESE ROLLED SANDWICHES

16 slices white bread, crusts removed	3 tablespoons sesame seed, toasted
1 (6-ounce) jar process cheese spread	Melted butter or margarine

Use a rolling pin to flatten slices of bread. Spread each with cheese; sprinkle with sesame seed. Roll each slice, jelly-roll fashion; brush with melted butter; cover with waxed paper or plastic wrap; chill for several hours.

Cut rolls in half crosswise and place on a cookie sheet, seam side down; bake at 425° for 10 minutes or until lightly browned. Yield: 32 sandwiches.

HAM CORNUCOPIAS

1 cup ground cooked ham	8 thin slices whole wheat
1 tablespoon finely chopped	bread
parsley	Softened butter or margarine
2 tablespoons mayonnaise	

Combine ham, parsley, and mayonnaise. Remove crusts from bread; roll lightly with a rolling pin. Spread with butter. Cut each slice in quarters. Place ¼ teaspoon of the ham mixture diagonally on each square of bread. Fold two opposite corners over and fasten with a wooden pick. Place on a cookie sheet, cover with waxed paper and a damp cloth, and chill for 30 minutes. Remove wooden picks before serving. Yield: 32 sandwiches.

STRAWBERRY CORNUCOPIAS

3 cups (1½ pints)	¼ cup finely chopped walnuts
strawberries	32 slices soft white bread
1 (8-ounce) package cream	(about two 1-pound loaves)
cheese, softened	
2 tablespoons powdered sugar	

Wash strawberries and hull; mash enough to measure 2 tablespoonfuls in a medium bowl; set remainder aside. Beat cream cheese and powdered sugar into mashed strawberries until smooth; stir in walnuts. Cut a round from center of each slice of bread with a 3-inch cookie cutter; roll each round thin with a rolling pin. Spread a rounded teaspoonful of cream cheese mixture over each; roll into a cornucopia shape. Halve remaining strawberries; tuck one half into end of each sandwich. Yield: 32 sandwiches.

Note: Sandwiches may be made up about an hour before serving. Place in a single layer on a cookie sheet or tray; cover tightly to prevent drying; chill. Add strawberry garnish just before serving so color doesn't run.

MUSHROOM SANDWICH LOAF

Trim crusts from a 1-pound loaf of day-old unsliced bread. Cut into 4 lengthwise slices. Spread softened butter and Chicken Salad Filling on one slice, butter and Deviled Salad Filling on second slice, and butter and Creamy Nut Filling on third slice. Arrange slices one on top of the other and cover with fourth slice. Frost loaf with creamy cheese mixture and garnish with nuts. Wrap loaf in a damp cloth and chill for several hours. Yield: about 12 sandwich slices.

Chicken Salad Filling:

½ cup cooked, diced chicken
¼ cup chopped celery
1 tablespoon minced onion
2 to 3 tablespoons
   mayonnaise
½ teaspoon salt

½ teaspoon curry powder
⅛ teaspoon pepper
1 (4-ounce) can sliced
   mushrooms, drained and
   chopped

Combine all ingredients; mix well. Set aside and later spread on bread slice.

Deviled Salad Filling:

1 (3-ounce) can deviled ham
2 to 3 tablespoons
   mayonnaise

2 tablespoons pickle relish
2 hard-cooked eggs, chopped

Combine all ingredients; mix well. Set aside and later spread on bread slice.

Creamy Nut Filling:

1 (3-ounce) package cream
   cheese, softened
4 to 6 tablespoons half-and
   half

1 cup chopped nuts
Pinch of salt

Combine all ingredients; mix well. Set aside and later spread on bread slice.

Frosting:

3 (3-ounce) packages cream
   cheese, softened

½ cup half-and-half
1 cup chopped nuts

Combine cream cheese and cream. Reserve nuts for garnish after sandwich loaf is frosted.

APRICOT-CREAM CHEESE DREAMS

1 (3-ounce) package cream
   cheese
Butter or margarine, softened

8 slices sandwich bread
⅓ cup cooked dried apricots,
   sweetened to taste

Let cream cheese soften at room temperature. Spread softened butter on bread slices. Spread mashed cream cheese on 4 slices of bread; spread other 4 slices with mashed apricots. Put slices together and cut sandwiches in rectangles or circles. Yield: about 16 sandwiches.

161

CHERRY-CHEESE SANDWICH SPREAD

1 (4-ounce) jar maraschino
cherries (red or green)

1 (3-ounce) package cream
cheese, softened

Drain cherries and dice very fine. Add to softened cream cheese and mix well. This filling may be used for open-faced sandwiches or made into 3-layered ribbon sandwiches. Yield: about 1½ cups.

SEAFOOD-CUCUMBER FILLING

1 cup crabmeat or chopped
cooked shrimp
⅓ cup grated peeled
cucumber, drained (press
moisture out between paper
towels)

2 teaspoons minced chives
1 to 2 teaspoons lemon juice
¼ teaspoon salt
⅛ teaspoon dillweed
¼ cup mayonnaise or
commercial sour cream

Combine all ingredients and chill thoroughly. Yield: about 1½ cups.
Note: If you make up sandwiches ahead of time, be sure to spread bread lightly with soft butter before filling sandwiches; the butter will prevent the filling from seeping in and causing sogginess.

SPICED APRICOT BREAD DAINTY SANDWICHES

1½ cups dried apricots, diced
1 cup sugar
½ teaspoon ground cloves
¼ teaspoon ground nutmeg
½ teaspoon ground cinnamon
½ teaspoon salt
6 tablespoons melted butter or
margarine

1 cup water
1 egg, beaten
2 cups all-purpose flour
1 teaspoon soda
1 cup chopped pecans or
walnuts (or mixed)
Sandwich Fillings

Combine apricots, sugar, spices, salt, butter, and water in a saucepan. Cook for 5 minutes and cool thoroughly. Add beaten egg, then flour mixed with soda. Stir in nuts, mix well, and turn into a greased 9- x 5- x 3-inch loafpan. Bake at 350° for 1 hour. Freezes beautifully. Yield: about 3 dozen small sandwiches.

For a party, chill bread, then slice thinly and make small, dainty sandwiches. For filling use one of the following:

Sandwich Fillings:

1. Softened cream cheese flavored with honey and lemon juice.
2. One cup chopped dates mixed with ¼ cup orange juice and ¼ cup finely chopped hazelnuts or walnuts.
3. Four ounces cream cheese mixed with 1 tablespoon grated orange rind, ¼ cup chopped seedless raisins, 2 tablespoons chopped pecans, and 2 tablespoons orange juice.

162

ORANGE CREAM CRESCENTS

1 cup apple jelly
1 (11-ounce) can mandarin
 orange sections, drained
1 (8-ounce) package cream
 cheese, softened

1 tablespoon grated orange
 rind
1 tablespoon milk
2 (8-ounce) cans orange-nut
 bread

Heat jelly just until melted in a small saucepan; remove from heat. Place orange sections, a few at a time, in jelly, turning to coat well. Lift out with a fork and place on a wire rack set over waxed paper; let stand until jelly sets. Blend cream cheese, orange rind, and milk in a small bowl. Slice bread into 16 rounds; halve each. Spread with cheese mixture; top each with 1 large or 2 small mandarin orange sections. Yield: 32 sandwiches.

DATE-STUFFED CHEESE BALLS

1 pound pitted dates
2 cups shredded Cheddar
 cheese
½ cup butter or margarine,
 softened

1 cup self-rising flour
1 teaspoon paprika

Cut dates in half; set aside. Combine cheese and butter in a mixing bowl. Stir in flour and paprika, and blend thoroughly. Chill dough 15 minutes. Put about 1 teaspoon of dough around each date half to form a ball.
 Place balls 3 inches apart on a lightly greased baking sheet; chill well. Bake at 400° for 15 to 20 minutes. Yield: about 4 dozen.
 Note: Cheese balls may be frozen before or after baking. If baked, cool thoroughly before freezing.

CELERY CHEESE SWIRLS

1 bunch celery
1 (8-ounce) package cream
 cheese, softened
½ cup shredded American
 cheese

1 tablespoon milk
1 tablespoon finely chopped
 onion
1 garlic clove, minced
Salt and pepper to taste

Separate celery into stalks; trim, and wash thoroughly. Combine cream cheese and American cheese; blend until smooth. Add milk, onion, garlic, salt, and pepper; mix until well blended.
 Spread cream cheese mixture on each celery stalk. Press 3 stalks together, and secure with rubber bands. Chill for 1 hour. Cut into ½- to 1-inch slices. Yield: about 3 dozen slices.

CRESCENT ROLLUPS

1 (8-ounce) can refrigerated crescent dinner rolls	½ teaspoon onion salt
½ cup commercial sour cream	½ pound bacon, cooked and crumbled

Separate dough into 8 triangles. Spread each with sour cream; sprinkle with onion salt and bacon.

Cut each triangle into 3 wedges; roll up each wedge to form small crescent rolls. Place on a greased cookie sheet, and bake at 375° for 15 minutes. Yield: 2 dozen.

TINY PARTY PUFFS

1 cup water	4 eggs
½ cup butter or margarine	Shrimp or Salmon Salad
1 cup all-purpose flour	Parsley or softened cream
Dash of salt	cheese

Bring water to boil. Add butter, stirring until melted. Add flour and salt all at once. Stir well until mixture is smooth and forms a soft ball. Cool mixture slightly. Add eggs, one at a time, beating well after each addition. After last addition, continue beating until mixture is shiny. Drop batter by teaspoonfuls onto a lightly greased cookie sheet to make 36 small puffs. Bake at 375° for 50 minutes. Allow to cool in a warm place, away from drafts. When cool, fill with Shrimp or Salmon Salad. Decorate with parsley or cream cheese in a flower design. Yield: 3 dozen.

Shrimp Salad:

1½ cups finely chopped cooked shrimp	2 teaspoons lemon juice
½ cup finely chopped celery	¾ cup mayonnaise or salad dressing
1 teaspoon caraway seeds	

Combine all ingredients and mix well. Refrigerate for at least an hour. Yield: enough filling for 3 dozen puffs.

Salmon Salad:

1½ cups flaked cooked salmon (1-pound can, drained)	½ cup mayonnaise or salad dressing
½ cup chopped nuts	Dash of hot pepper sauce
¼ cup finely chopped green pepper	

Combine all ingredients and mix well. Refrigerate for at least 1 hour. Yield: enough filling for 3 dozen puffs.

GRAND MARNIER PUFFS

1 cup water	Crème Pâtissière
½ cup butter or margarine	Powdered sugar
¼ teaspoon salt	Orange and lemon slices
1 cup all-purpose flour	(optional)
4 eggs	

Combine water, butter, and salt in a saucepan; heat to boiling point. Remove from heat; add flour all at once, stirring vigorously until mixture leaves sides of pan and forms a ball around spoon. (If a ball does not form almost immediately, place saucepan over low heat and beat briskly for a few minutes.) Cool 5 minutes.

Add eggs, one at a time, beating until mixture is smooth and glossy after each addition. Drop batter by rounded teaspoonfuls onto a greased baking sheet, spacing about 2 inches apart. Bake at 425° for 15 minutes. Reduce temperature to 350°, and bake an additional 8 minutes. (Inside should be dry and firm.) Cool.

Just before serving, cut top off each puff; fill bottom of each with Crème Pâtissière. Replace tops, and sprinkle with powdered sugar. Garnish with orange and lemon slices, if desired. Yield: about 3 dozen.

Crème Pâtissière:

¾ cup sugar	1½ teaspoons vanilla extract
7 egg yolks	Grated rind of 3 oranges
⅓ cup all-purpose flour	1 to 2 tablespoons Grand
Pinch of salt	Marnier or other
2 cups milk, scalded	orange-flavored liqueur

Combine sugar and egg yolks, beating until pale yellow and fluffy. Combine flour and salt; gradually add to yolk mixture, beating well. Very gradually stir milk into yolk mixture; pour into a heavy saucepan. Cook over low heat until thickened, stirring constantly.

Remove custard from heat; stir in vanilla, orange rind, and Grand Marnier. Cover with plastic wrap, pressing onto surface to prevent formation of a crust. Chill well. Yield: about 3 cups.

• *Separate raw eggs while still cold from the refrigerator, but let whites come to room temperature if they need to be stiffly beaten.*

• *Whenever a recipe calls for both orange juice and rind, wash and grate the orange before juicing.*

• *Instead of using an ice block for your punch bowl, try this: Prepare a mixture of orange juice and any other fruit juice desired. The mixture should be quite strong. Pour into a mold or plastic container, and add strawberries or other fruit if desired; freeze. Place the frozen juice block in your punch bowl and pour punch over it. The block will prevent punch from becoming watery during a long serving period and will add to the flavor of the punch.*

ALMOND FINGERS

1 cup butter, softened	1 teaspoon almond extract
½ cup powdered sugar	2 cups chopped toasted
1½ cups all-purpose flour	almonds
Pinch of salt	Powdered sugar

Cream butter and sugar thoroughly in large bowl of electric mixer. Add flour mixed with salt; blend well; beat in almond extract. Stir in almonds; chill about an hour for easier handling.

To bake, pinch off about a tablespoon of mixture and roll between palms of hands into a 2-inch-long cylinder about ½ inch thick. Place on lightly greased cookie sheets and bake at 325° for 20 minutes or until very lightly browned. Remove cookies to a flat pan onto which you have sifted powdered sugar, then sift more sugar over top of cookies. Store in an airtight container with waxed paper between layers. Freezes well. Yield: about 6 dozen.

CHOCOLATE CHERRIES

1 (7¼-ounce) package vanilla wafers, finely crushed	30 maraschino cherries with stems
½ cup powdered sugar	2 (6-ounce) packages
½ cup chopped walnuts	semisweet chocolate
¼ cup boiling water	morsels
2 tablespoons butter or margarine	Flaked coconut (optional)
1 tablespoon light corn syrup	Multicolored sprinkles (optional)
2 teaspoons instant coffee granules	Chocolate sprinkles (optional)
	Chopped nuts (optional)

Combine vanilla wafer crumbs, powdered sugar, and walnuts. Combine water, butter, corn syrup, and instant coffee; add to first mixture. Shape approximately ½ tablespoon of this mixture around each cherry. Cover and refrigerate for at least 1 hour.

Melt chocolate over warm water. Holding stem, dip coated cherries into chocolate, coating carefully and completely. Place on wire rack over waxed paper. After about 5 minutes, garnish with coconut, sprinkles, or nuts, if desired. Refrigerate until chocolate has hardened. Yield: 2½ dozen.

CREAM WAFERS

1 cup butter or margarine, softened	2 cups all-purpose flour
⅓ cup whipping cream	Sugar
	Cream Filling

Combine butter, cream and flour thoroughly; chill. Divide dough into thirds. (Keep remainder in refrigerator until ready to roll.) Roll ⅓ of dough ⅛ inch thick on floured cloth-covered board. Cut with 1½-inch round cutter. Place rounds on waxed paper that is heavily covered with sugar. Turn each round with spatula so both sides are coated with sugar. Place on ungreased cookie sheet; prick each about 4 times with a fork. Bake at 375° for 7 to 9 minutes. Cool; put 2 cookies together with Cream Filling. Yield: about 5 dozen double cookies.

Cream Filling:

¼ cup butter or margarine,
   softened
¾ cup powdered sugar

1 egg yolk
1 teaspoon vanilla extract
Food coloring (optional)

Combine butter, powdered sugar, egg yolk, and vanilla extract; mix until smooth. Tint with food coloring, if desired. Yield: about 1 cup.

HOLIDAY LOG CAKE

¾ teaspoon baking powder
¼ teaspoon salt
4 eggs, at room temperature
¾ cup sugar
¾ cup all-purpose flour
¼ cup cocoa
1 teaspoon vanilla extract
2 to 3 tablespoons powdered
   sugar
2 cups sweetened whipped
   cream

3 (1-ounce) squares
   unsweetened chocolate
¼ cup butter or margarine
1 tablespoon instant coffee
   granules
Dash of salt
⅓ cup boiling water
About 2½ cups sifted
   powdered sugar
Candied cherries

Grease a 15- x 10- x 1-inch pan; line with waxed paper and grease lightly. Set aside.

Combine baking powder, ¼ teaspoon salt, and eggs in mixing bowl; beat at medium speed of electric mixer. Add sugar gradually, beating until thick and light colored. Fold in flour, cocoa, and vanilla.

Spread mixture evenly into prepared pan. Bake at 400° for 13 minutes or until surface springs back when gently pressed.

Sift 2 to 3 tablespoons powdered sugar in a 15- x 10-inch rectangle on a linen towel. Turn cake out on sugar; remove waxed paper from cake. Trim crisp edges, if necessary. Starting with the short end, carefully roll cake and towel, jelly-roll fashion. Cool thoroughly on wire rack. Unroll; spread with whipped cream, and reroll. Chill.

Melt chocolate in top of a double boiler; blend in butter, coffee, salt, and boiling water, stirring until smooth. Cool to lukewarm. Stir in about 2½ cups powdered sugar to make a spreading consistency. Spread frosting evenly over cake. Mark with tines of a fork to resemble bark of a tree. Decorate with candied cherries. Refrigerate until serving time. Yield: 8 to 10 servings.

Photograph for this recipe on page 154

PARTY MACAROON MUFFINS

1 cup butter, softened	½ teaspoon almond extract
½ cup sugar	2 cups all-purpose flour
1 egg	Almond Macaroon Filling
½ teaspoon vanilla extract	

Cream butter and sugar thoroughly in large bowl of electric mixer. Beat in egg, flavorings, and flour. Drop by teaspoonfuls into tiny greased muffin cups, pressing dough over bottom and up around sides. Chill. Fill little cups with Almond Macaroon Filling. Bake at 325° for 25 to 30 minutes. Freezes well. Yield: 3 dozen.

Almond Macaroon Filling:

2 eggs	1 teaspoon almond extract
½ cup sugar	
1¼ cups finely chopped blanched almonds	

Beat eggs until light and fluffy. Gradually beat in sugar until well blended. Fold in almonds and almond extract. Yield: filling for 3 dozen muffins.

MARZIPAN CUPCAKES

⅓ cup butter	1 cup all-purpose flour
¼ cup powdered sugar	Filling
1 egg yolk	Frosting
¼ teaspoon almond extract	

Cream butter and sugar well in bowl of electric mixer; add egg yolk and almond extract; mix well. Blend in flour, then chill for about an hour for easier handling. Pinch off marble-size pieces and press into bottom and sides of tiny ungreased muffin tins. Bake at 375° for 7 to 8 minutes. Yield: 3 dozen.

Filling:

⅓ cup butter	2 eggs
½ (8-ounce) can almond paste	½ teaspoon almond extract
½ cup sugar	

Cream butter with almond paste until well blended; beat in ½ cup sugar thoroughly. Blend in eggs and ½ teaspoon almond extract. Spoon into each baked shell, then bake at 350° for 20 minutes. While tarts bake, prepare Frosting. Drizzle over outer edges of warm cakes. Bake cupcakes ahead of time and freeze. Yield: filling for 3 dozen cupcakes.

Frosting:

¾ cup powdered sugar   ¼ teaspoon almond extract
Orange or lemon juice to taste

Combine all ingredients; blend well. Yield: frosting for 3 dozen cupcakes.

QUICK PETITS FOURS

Make cake using pound cake mix or bake a pound cake in two 8-inch square pans. Cut slices about ¾ inch thick. Then if desired, cut slices in fancy shapes with small cutters. Put together sandwich-fashion with jam or jelly between.

To frost and decorate, put Petits Fours on rack with tray underneath to catch drippings. Spoon Petits Fours Frosting over cakes until coated, scraping frosting up from tray to reuse. When firm, decorate, using a pastry tube, with Decorating Frosting. If you have no pastry tube, you can improvise one with a sheet of stiff white paper. Freezes beautifully. Two 8-inch square cakes will yield about 50 small squares.

Petits Fours Frosting:

1 cup sugar   Flavoring (½ teaspoon vanilla,
Dash of cream of tartar   almond, rum, brandy—any
⅛ teaspoon salt   flavor you like)
½ cup water   Food coloring (optional)
Sifted powdered sugar

Bring sugar, cream of tartar, salt, and water to a boil; cook to 236° on a candy thermometer (soft-ball stage). Cool to lukewarm (100°). Gradually beat in enough powdered sugar until thick enough to almost hold its shape. Add flavoring. Divide into four parts. If desired, leave one part white and tint others pink, yellow, green, etc.

Decorating Frosting:

Mix until smooth two parts powdered sugar to one part butter or margarine. Flavor and color as desired. Or buy tubes of colored frostings which are available with decorating tips to fit the tubes.

ASSORTED PETITS FOURS

Fondant:

2 cups boiling water	**¼ teaspoon cream of tartar**
6 cups sugar	

Put all ingredients in a deep heavy saucepan; stir until sugar has dissolved, then cook quickly without stirring until syrup reaches 236° on a candy thermometer (or to soft-ball stage when a little is dropped into cold water). Occasionally wash off crystals that form on sides of pan, using a brush dipped in cold water.

Pour onto a buttered marble slab, large pan, or platter. Cool until lukewarm; then, using a spatula, pull sides into middle repeatedly until mixture turns white and thick. Let stand 5 minutes; then knead with buttered hands until creamy enough to form a firm ball. At first it will be crumbly, but butter hands heavily and often. Store Fondant in a tightly-covered container for at least 2 days before using. Yield: 1 quart. This is too much for the recipe that follows, but it keeps well, refrigerated or frozen, and it's advisable to have enough on hand for more than one batch of cakes.

To prepare Fondant for frosting cakes, warm 1 or 2 cups slowly over hot water (do not allow water to boil or Fondant will lose its shine and become dull and unattractive). If you wish, tint desired shade with a few drops of food coloring. Stir in flavoring to taste, such as vanilla, rum, almond, or other extracts. Thin Fondant to heavy cream consistency by adding a few drops of hot water at a time.

Chocolate Fondant:

Melt 2 (1-ounce) squares unsweetened chocolate; cool. Add it to 1 cup Fondant and stir mixture over low flame until it is warm to the touch. Add ½ teaspoon vanilla and thin to the right consistency with a little warm water.

Pound Cake:

Pound cake is most satisfactory for Pettis Fours as it cuts cleanly and does not crumble.

1 cup butter	**1 teaspoon vanilla extract**
1 cup sugar	**2¼ cups all-purpose flour**
6 eggs	**⅛ teaspoon salt**

Cream butter thoroughly in large bowl of electric mixer. Beat in sugar until mixture is light and fluffy. Add eggs one at a time, blending well after each addition. Add vanilla, then mixed dry ingredients. Butter two 8-inch square pans; line bottoms with waxed paper, butter the paper, then dust with flour. Pour equal amount of batter in each pan and spread evenly. Bake at 300° for about 40 minutes or until cakes test done. Cool in pans about 5 minutes, invert onto wire racks, and peel off paper. Let cool and if desired, wrap in heavy-duty aluminum foil and freeze until ready to use.

To complete the Petits Fours: Trim edges from cakes and cut into

1¼-inch squares or rectangles about 2 x 1¼ inches. The little cakes may now be frosted; however, the most elegant Petits Fours are filled with a butter cream before frosting. Here's the way: Cut a ⅓-inch slice from top of each cake and lay it aside. Hollow out the center of cake, fill with Butter Cream Filling, and replace top. Place cakes on a wire rack on a pan and work quickly to coat top and sides with Fondant. Decorate tops with nuts, chocolate shots, silver dragées, or candied fruit. Put in paper bonbon cups and arrange beautifully on silver tray.

Basic Butter Cream Filling:

¾ cup sugar	1 cup butter, softened
¼ cup water	Favorite extract or liqueur
⅛ teaspoon cream of tartar	(optional)
5 egg yolks	

Combine sugar, water, and cream of tartar in saucepan; stir until dissolved. Cook rapidly to 250° on candy thermometer or until syrup spins a thread. Meanwhile, beat egg yolks until very light. Pour syrup in a slow steady stream into yolks, beating constantly until mixture is thick and cool. Whip butter and blend thoroughly into yolk mixture; flavor with any extract or liqueur desired. Keep at room temperature to use immediately or store covered in refrigerator, or freeze, for later use. Yield: about 2 cups, enough for about 50 square Petits Fours or 30 rectangular ones cut from the two square 8-inch pound cakes.

Filling Variations: For Orange Butter Cream, blend ½ cup Basic Butter Cream with 2 teaspoons thawed frozen orange juice concentrate and ¼ teaspoon grated orange rind.

For Mocha Butter Cream, dissolve 2 teaspoons cocoa and ½ teaspoon instant coffee granules in 1½ teaspoons hot water. Blend with ½ cup Basic Butter Cream Filling.

STRAWBERRY CANDIES

1 (15-ounce) can sweetened condensed milk	1 cup finely ground almonds
	1 tablespoon sugar
1 pound finely ground coconut	1 teaspoon vanilla extract
2 (3-ounce) packages strawberry-flavored gelatin, divided	1 (4½-ounce) can green decorator icing

Combine milk, coconut, 1 package gelatin, almonds, sugar, and vanilla; mix well. Shape mixture into strawberries. Roll candies in remaining gelatin, coating thoroughly. Let candies dry until firm. Make leaves with icing on top of candies. Store in a covered container. Yield: about 48.

Photograph for this recipe on page 154

Bloody Marys (page 174); Orange-Champagne Cocktail (page 174); Pep Shake (page 176); Christmas Eggnog (page 175)

beverages

On cold winter evenings, welcome your friends with a bracing cup of one of our hot beverages. They are fun to fix and are guaranteed to take the chill off. Some can even serve as dessert or take the place of after-dinner coffee at your next dinner party.

A tall, frosty glass of a refreshing beverage is one of the nicest ways to welcome guests. Make it special by garnishing with fresh mint, strawberries, or a slice of orange, lemon, or lime. For an added cool touch, frost the glasses by dipping the rims in lemon or lime juice, then in powdered sugar.

If you are looking for light refreshers, you'll find some here that are deliciously cooling. You can mix them by the glass or pitcherful to sip while you relax in the shade.

Most of the delicious beverages can be prepared ahead of time, at least in part. Just store them in the refrigerator or freezer until guests arrive, and you have instant hospitality.

BLOODY MARYS

1½ cups tomato-clam juice
½ cup vodka
1 tablespoon plus 1 teaspoon
  Worcestershire sauce
Juice of 1 lime

3 to 4 dashes of hot sauce
Celery salt
Salt and pepper
2 celery stalks (optional)

Combine first 5 ingredients in a pitcher, mixing well. Pour over ice cubes; sprinkle each serving with celery salt, salt, and pepper. Garnish each with a stalk of celery, if desired. Yield: 2 servings.

Photograph for this recipe on page 172

MOCK PINK CHAMPAGNE

½ cup sugar
1½ cups water
2 cups cranberry juice
1 cup pineapple juice

½ cup orange juice
2 (7-ounce) bottles lemon-lime
  carbonated beverage

Boil sugar and water until sugar dissolves; cool. Stir in cranberry juice, pineapple juice, and orange juice. Chill. Just before serving, add carbonated beverage. Yield: 14 servings.

ORANGE-CHAMPAGNE COCKTAIL

3½ cups champagne, chilled
1 (28-ounce) bottle ginger ale,
  chilled

2 cups orange juice, chilled
Fresh fruit (optional)

Combine champagne, ginger ale, and orange juice in a pitcher or punch bowl; stir gently. Garnish with fresh fruit, if desired. Yield: 9 cups.

Photograph for this recipe on page 172

CAFÉ DE OLLA

Ground coffee
Water
3 whole cloves
3 whole peppercorns
5 (1-inch) strips lemon peel
6 (1-inch) strips orange peel

¼ teaspoon ground cinnamon
Rum to taste
8 teaspoons brown sugar
Whipped cream
Ground nutmeg

Put enough coffee and water in percolator to make 8 cups coffee of desired strength. Before perking, add the following to coffee in basket: cloves, peppercorns, lemon peel, orange peel, and cinnamon. Perk to taste.

Pour coffee into mugs; add rum to taste. Stir 1 teaspoon brown sugar into each mug. After coffee stops swirling, top with whipped cream and sprinkle with nutmeg. Yield: 8 servings.

BRAZILIAN COFFEE

⅓ cup cocoa
1 teaspoon ground cinnamon
½ teaspoon salt
1 (14-ounce) can sweetened
  condensed milk

1 quart water
1½ cups strong coffee
Cinnamon sticks
Ground nutmeg

Combine cocoa, cinnamon, and salt in a 3-quart saucepan. Add sweetened condensed milk, stirring until smooth. Place pan over medium heat; gradually stir in water and coffee. Heat thoroughly (do not boil). Garnish each cup with a cinnamon stick, and sprinkle with nutmeg. Refrigerate leftovers. Yield: about 7 cups.

Note: Add ½ cup brandy and ¼ cup light rum along with water and coffee, if desired.

Photograph for this recipe on page 5

CHRISTMAS EGGNOG

1 cup sugar
1 quart half-and-half
8 eggs, separated
1 to 1½ pints bourbon, rum,
  or brandy

Ground nutmeg
Whipped cream

Prepare at least a day before you plan to serve. Mix sugar and half-and-half. Beat egg whites and add to the sugar and cream mixture. Fold in until egg whites cannot be seen. Add beaten egg yolks and mix well. Slowly stir in bourbon, rum, or brandy. Cover and put in refrigerator. To serve, ladle into cups, sprinkle with nutmeg, and add a spoon of whipped cream to each cup. Yield 15 to 20 servings.

Photograph for this recipe on page 172

PARTY PERFECT EGGNOG

6 eggs
½ cup light corn syrup
¼ teaspoon ground ginger
¼ teaspoon ground cloves
¼ teaspoon ground cinnamon
¼ teaspoon ground nutmeg

2 quarts orange juice, chilled
½ cup lemon juice, chilled
1 quart vanilla ice cream
1 quart ginger ale, chilled
Ground nutmeg

Beat eggs well. Mix in syrup, ginger, cloves, cinnamon, and nutmeg, Stir in orange juice and lemon juice. Cut ice cream into chunks the size of small eggs; put into a large punch bowl.

Pour ginger ale over ice cream. Stir in egg mixture. Sprinkle with nutmeg. Yield: 6 quarts.

SPICED LEMONADE

¾ cup sugar
4¾ cups water, divided
12 whole cloves

7 cinnamon sticks, divided
Juice of 6 lemons
Lemon slices

Combine sugar and ¾ cup water; boil about 5 minutes. Add cloves and 1 cinnamon stick; cook 5 minutes over medium heat. Strain into pitcher.

Add lemon juice and remaining 4 cups water. Chill. Serve over ice. Garnish each glass with a lemon slice; use remaining cinnamon sticks for stirrers. Yield: 6 servings.

ORANGE SPARKLER

1 (12-ounce) can frozen
  orange juice concentrate,
  thawed and undiluted
3¾ cups water
2 tablespoons lime juice

4 teaspoons rum flavoring
1 (32-ounce) bottle
  lemon-lime carbonated
  beverage, chilled
Orange slices

Combine orange juice concentrate, water, lime juice, and rum flavoring in a large pitcher; stir until well mixed. Add lemon-lime carbonated beverage. Serve over ice, and garnish with orange slices. Yield: 10 servings.

PEP SHAKE

1 (16-ounce) can sliced
  peaches
1 cup vanilla ice cream

2 eggs
Fresh mint sprigs (optional)

Combine all ingredients except mint sprigs in container of electric blender; process until smooth. Pour into chilled glasses; garnish each with a sprig of mint, if desired. Yield: 3¼ cups.

Photograph for this recipe on page 172

SPARKLING PINK LADY

3 cups pineapple juice,
  chilled
1 cup gin

¼ cup grenadine
Juice of 1 lemon
Crushed ice (optional)

Combine all ingredients, and mix well. Shake with crushed ice, and strain into cocktail glasses (may be served over crushed ice, if desired). Yield 6 to 8 servings.

APPLE BLOSSOM PUNCH

3 quarts apple juice
3 (12-ounce) cans frozen
   orange juice concentrate

3 quarts ginger ale
Ice
Fresh orange slices

Combine fruit juices and ginger ale. Pour over block of ice. Float orange slices on top of punch. Yield: 50 servings.

CRANBERRY PUNCH

3 quarts cranberry juice
   cocktail
1½ quarts orange juice
1½ cups water

2½ cups lemon juice
3 cups pineapple juice
3 cups sugar
Lemon slices

Combine all ingredients except lemon slices and blend well. Chill in refrigerator. Pour into a punch bowl with an ice ring and lemon slices. Yield: 50 servings.

Party Punch (page 181); Sparkling Pink Lady (page 176); Orange Sparkler (page 176); Spiced Lemonade (page 176); Sangría Southern (page 186)

EASY CRANBERRY PUNCH

1 quart cranberry juice cocktail	1 quart pineapple-grapefruit juice
1½ cups sugar	2 quarts ginger ale, chilled

Slowly add cranberry juice to sugar; stir until sugar dissolves. Add pineapple-grapefruit juice; chill. Pour into punch bowls; add chilled ginger ale. Yield: 32 servings.

FRUIT PUNCH

2 (6-ounce) cans frozen orange juice concentrate	1 cup pineapple juice
1 (6-ounce) can frozen lemonade concentrate	¼ cup cherry juice (optional)
	2 quarts ginger ale, chilled
	Ice

Mix fruit juices; cover and let stand for 12 hours or more in refrigerator. Add cold ginger ale to juices just before serving. Serve over crushed ice or freeze half the ginger ale in ice cube trays. Yield: 24 servings.

HOLIDAY FRUIT PUNCH

2 quarts water	1 quart water
¼ cup loose tea	Ice
2 cups sugar	1 quart ginger ale
2 cups lemon juice	1 lemon, sliced
1 quart orange juice	2 limes, sliced
1½ quarts cranberry juice	Maraschino cherries

Bring 2 quarts water to a full rolling boil. Immediately pour over the tea; brew for 5 minutes. Strain. Set aside to cool at room temperature. Combine with sugar, fruit juices, and 1 quart water. Chill. Just before serving, pour over a large piece of ice or ice cubes; then add ginger ale. Garnish with lemon and lime slices and cherries. Yield: 25 servings.

GOLDEN GATE PUNCH

2½ cups sugar	1 quart strained orange juice
1 cup water	1¼ cups lemon juice
2 (18-ounce) cans pineapple juice	2 quarts chilled ginger ale
2 cups strained lime juice	Colored ice cubes

Combine sugar and water; heat to boiling. Cool. Combine fruit juices. Add cooled sugar syrup. Chill. Just before serving, add ginger ale and colored ice cubes. To make colored cubes, blend food coloring with water before freezing. Yield: 5 quarts.

GRAPE PUNCH

2 cups grape juice
1½ cups orange juice
¾ cup sugar
1 cup water

Ice cubes
3 (7-ounce) bottles ginger ale
1 lemon, sliced

Pour fruit juices into a 2-quart pitcher. Add sugar and stir until dissolved. Add water and ice cubes. Let stand for a few minutes in refrigerator. Pour equal amounts into 16 tall glasses in which there are a couple of ice cubes. Then fill to top with ginger ale and garnish with lemon slices. Yield: 16 servings.

HOLIDAY PUNCH

Juice of 2 limes
Juice of 1 lemon
3 (6-ounce) cans frozen
　orange juice concentrate
1 (6-ounce) can frozen lemon
　juice concentrate
1 (6-ounce) can frozen lime
　juice concentrate

1 (18-ounce) can pineapple
　juice
½ teaspoon salt
1½ quarts water
1 quart chilled ginger ale
1 pint vodka
Red food coloring (optional)
Ice

Several hours ahead mix together the fruit juices, salt, and water; place in a covered container in the refrigerator to chill.

At serving time, combine above mixture with ginger ale and vodka. Stir in food coloring, if desired. Serve over a block of ice in a punch bowl. Yield: 25 servings.

MINTED PUNCH

1½ cups packed mint leaves
　and stems
2 cups water
2 (12-ounce) cans frozen
　lemonade concentrate,
　thawed and undiluted

3 (28-ounce) bottles ginger
　ale, chilled
Strawberries
Sprigs of mint

Bruise mint leaves, and place in a medium saucepan. Cover mint with 2 cups water, and bring to a boil. Remove from heat, and let stand about 15 minutes; strain.

Combine mint liquid, lemonade, and ginger ale in a large bowl. Serve in tall glasses; garnish each with strawberries and a sprig of mint. Yield: 1 gallon.

Open-House Punch (below)

OPEN-HOUSE PUNCH

2½ cups bourbon
1 (6-ounce) can frozen orange
  juice concentrate, thawed
  and undiluted
2 (6-ounce) cans frozen
  lemonade concentrate,
  thawed and undiluted

⅔ cup lemon juice
7 (10-ounce) bottles
  lemon-lime carbonated
  beverage, chilled
Ice cubes
Lemon slices
Mint sprigs

Combine bourbon, orange juice, lemonade, and lemon juice; stir well. Add carbonated beverage and ice cubes. Garnish with lemon slices and mint. Yield: 3 quarts.

PARTY PUNCH

2 cups sugar	¾ cup lemon juice
2 (3-ounce) packages	2 cups cold water
lime-flavored gelatin	2 (28-ounce) bottles ginger
1 quart boiling water	ale, chilled
1 (46-ounce) can pineapple	Lime slices
juice	

Dissolve sugar and gelatin in boiling water; add fruit juices and cold water. Pour into two 2-quart containers; freeze.

Remove fruit juice mixture from freezer 2 to 3 hours before serving. Just before serving, add ginger ale; mix well. Garnish with lime slices. Yield: about 40 (4-ounce) servings.

Photograph for this recipe on page 177

PICNIC PUNCH

2½ cups apricot nectar	1 cup sugar syrup
2½ cups pineapple juice	Ice cubes
1 cup lemon juice	2 quarts ginger ale

Combine fruit juices and sugar syrup; pour over ice in a punch bowl or a vacuum bottle, blending well. Add ginger ale when ready to serve, stirring gently to mix. Yield: about 16 servings.

PUNCHMELON

1 large watermelon	Ice
2 cups orange juice	2 quarts bottled lemon-lime
2 cups lemon juice	beverage, chilled
1 (6-ounce) bottle grenadine	1 orange, sliced
syrup	1 lemon, sliced

With melon standing on end, cut a thin slice off side so it will sit level. Remove top third of melon. Using a coffee cup as a guide, trace scallops around top outside edge. With a sharp knife, carve scalloped edge, following tracing; scoop out fruit, leaving just a trace of red showing in bowl of melon; use scraped-out melon as desired. Chill melon bowl.

Combine orange juice, lemon juice, and grenadine; chill. When ready to serve, place a small block of ice, or ice cubes, in melon bowl. Pour juices over ice; pour lemon-lime beverage down side of melon bowl into juice mixture. Float orange and lime slices on top of punch. Yield: 3½ quarts.

PINEAPPLE-CRANBERRY PUNCH

1 quart cranberry juice	1 quart sparkling water or
2 cups orange juice	ginger ale
¼ cup lemon juice	Ice
1 quart pineapple sherbet	

Combine cranberry juice, orange juice, and lemon juice; beat in pineapple sherbet; then chill. Just before serving, slowly pour in sparkling water. Pour over cracked ice and serve immediately. Yield: 14 to 16 servings.

RED VELVET PUNCH

2 quarts cranberry juice cocktail	1 (6-ounce) can frozen lemon juice
1 (6-ounce) can frozen orange juice	2 cups brandy
1 (6-ounce) can frozen pineapple juice	Ice
	2 (4/5-quart) bottles white champagne

Combine juices and brandy; mix well and pour over a block of ice in a punch bowl. Add champagne. Yield: about 30 servings.

SEA FOAM PUNCH

½ cup sugar	1 pint vanilla ice cream
1 quart cold water	2 (7-ounce) bottles lemon-lime
1 (½-ounce) envelope	carbonated beverage,
unsweetened lemon-lime	chilled
soft drink powder	

Place sugar and water in large punch bowl. Add soft drink powder and stir until powder dissolves. Add vanilla ice cream, one spoonful at a time. Pour in carbonated beverage. Serve immediately. Yield: about 16 servings.

SPICED PUNCH

1 (3-ounce) package cherry-flavored gelatin	6 whole sticks cinnamon
1 quart boiling water, divided	3 tablespoons tea leaves
3 cups sugar	Juice of 12 lemons
3½ quarts water	1 (46-ounce) can pineapple juice
20 whole cloves	Lemon slices

Dissolve gelatin in 2 cups boiling water. Add sugar and 3½ quarts cold water, stirring until sugar is dissolved.

Combine cloves, cinnamon, and tea leaves in 2 cups boiling water, and let steep 20 minutes; strain. Add to gelatin mixture; stir in lemon juice and pineapple juice. Serve hot or cold, and garnish with lemon slices. Yield: 4½ quarts.

Spiced Punch (page 182)

SUNSHINE PUNCH

1 (46-ounce) can orange-pineapple juice, chilled	Ice cubes Orange slices Lemon slices
1 (28-ounce) bottle ginger ale or lemon-lime carbonated beverage, chilled	

Combine juice and ginger ale in a punch bowl. Serve over ice cubes, and garnish with orange and lemon slices. Yield: 8 servings.

Note: For delicious variations, 1 pint of pineapple sherbet or vodka to taste may be added to punch.

183

GOLDEN TEA PUNCH

3 cups boiling water	2¼ cups lemon juice
10 tea bags or 10 teaspoons tea leaves	1¼ cups orange juice
24 whole cloves	3 cups sugar
1 (3-inch) stick cinnamon, crumbled	1 gallon cold water
	Ice
	Orange and lemon slices

Pour boiling water over tea bags, whole cloves, and crumbled stick cinnamon. Cover; steep for 5 minutes. Strain and cool. Add lemon juice, orange juice, and sugar, stirring until sugar is dissolved. Add cold water. Pour into ice-filled punch bowl. Garnish with orange and lemon slices. Yield: 50 servings.

HOSPITALITY TEA PUNCH

2 quarts boiling water	1½ quarts grape juice
15 tea bags or 5 tablespoons loose tea	2 cups sugar
2 cups lemon juice	2 quarts cold water
1 quart orange juice	1 quart ginger ale
	Ice cubes

Pour boiling water over tea. Steep for 3 to 5 minutes and remove tea bags, or strain tea leaves. Cool tea. Stir in remaining ingredients except ginger ale and ice. Add ginger ale and ice cubes just before serving. Yield: 2 gallons.

Photograph for this recipe on page 9

WASSAIL PUNCH

1 gallon apple cider	24 whole cloves
1 quart orange juice	4 sticks cinnamon
1 cup lemon juice	1 cup sugar
1 quart pineapple juice	

Mix all ingredients and simmer for 10 minutes. Remove cinnamon and cloves. Serve warm in punch cups. Yield: 1½ gallons.

Note: For a festive punch bowl, float small oranges that have been precooked about 10 minutes. Stick several cloves in each orange.

HOT BUTTERED RUM

1 pound butter, softened	1 quart vanilla ice cream, softened
1 pound light brown sugar	Light rum
1 pound powdered sugar	Whipped cream
2 teaspoons ground cinnamon	Cinnamon sticks
2 teaspoons ground nutmeg	

Combine butter, sugars, and spices; beat until light and fluffy. Add ice cream, stirring until well blended. Spoon mixture into a 2-quart freezer container; freeze.

To serve, thaw slightly. Place 3 tablespoons butter mixture and 1 jigger rum in a large mug; fill with boiling water. Stir well. (Any unused butter mixture can be refrozen.) Top with whipped cream, and serve with cinnamon stick stirrers. Yield: about 25 cups.

Hot Buttered Rum (page 184)

QUICK SANGRÍA

2 (6-ounce) cans frozen pink
   lemonade concentrate,
   thawed and undiluted
4½ cups rosé, chilled
Juice of 1 lime

2 cups club soda, chilled
1 lemon, thinly sliced
1 orange, thinly sliced

Combine lemonade, rosé, and lime juice; stir until well blended. Slowly stir in soda. Garnish with lemon and orange slices. Yield: 6 to 8 servings.

SANGRÍA SOUTHERN

1 lemon, thinly sliced
1 orange, thinly sliced
1 lime, thinly sliced
Sugar
1 jigger Triple Sec or other
   orange liqueur

1 (4/5-quart) bottle dry red
   wine
½ cup club soda, chilled
Ice
Additional lime slices

Remove seeds from sliced fruit; place slices in glass pitcher, and add 1 to 2 tablespoons sugar. Do not add too much sugar until wine has been added. Allow to stand a few minutes.

Add Triple Sec to sliced fruit; stir with wooden spoon, bruising fruit to extract juices. Add wine; more sugar may be added, if desired. Chill. Just before serving, add club soda. Serve over ice, and garnish with additional lime slices. Yield: 6 to 8 servings.

Photograph for this recipe on page 177

VODKA SLUSH

1 (6-ounce) can frozen orange
   juice concentrate, thawed
   and undiluted
2 (6-ounce) cans frozen
   lemonade concentrate,
   thawed and undiluted
2 (6-ounce) cans frozen
   limeade concentrate,
   thawed and undiluted

1 cup sugar
3½ cups water
2 cups vodka
2 (28-ounce) bottles
   lemon-lime carbonated
   beverage, chilled

Combine first 6 ingredients, mixing well. Freeze 48 hours, stirring occasionally. For each serving, spoon ¾ cup frozen mixture into a tall glass; fill with carbonated beverage. Serve at once. Yield: about 16 (8-ounce) servings.

INDEX